P9-DFX-782

Unbought and Unbossed

Shirley Chisholm

Unbought and Unbossed

Houghton Mifflin Company Boston

SEVENTH PRINTING C

Library of Congress Catalog Card Number: 79-120834
ISBN: 0-395-10932-9
Printed in the United States of America

The author is grateful to the editors
of *The Black Politician* for permission
to quote from an article by Julian Bond
which appeared in the Winter 1969 issue.

To Conrad, for his deep understanding

Grateful acknowledgment for assistance in the preparation of this book is due to Wesley McD. Holder, for his tireless efforts and loyalty; to Samuel Korb, for his legal assistance; to my Washington and Brooklyn office staffs; to Lee Hickling, for research and editing aid; to Joan Middleton, for typing the manuscript.

Contents

IV
LOOKING AHEAD

Introduction

THERE ARE 435 members of the House of Representatives and 417 are white males. Ten of the others are women and nine are black. I belong to both of these minorities, which makes it add up right. That makes me a celebrity, a kind of side show attraction. I was the first American citizen to be elected to Congress in spite of the double drawbacks of being female and having skin darkened by melanin.

When you put it that way, it sounds like a foolish reason for fame. In a just and free society it would be foolish. That I am a national figure because I was the first person in 192 years to be at once a congressman, black, and a woman proves, I would think, that our society is not yet either just or free.

Sometimes the media make me feel like a monkey in a cage. As soon as I was elected, the newspapers and networks started to besiege me. The first question was almost always, "How does it feel?" Naturally, it feels good. I am proud and honored that the people of my district believed in me enough to choose me to represent them. My Twelfth Congressional District of Brooklyn is mostly composed of poor neighborhoods with all the problems of poverty in an aggravated form:

slum housing, high unemployment, too few medical services, high crime rate, neglected schools — the whole list. About 69 percent of my people are black and Puerto Rican. The rest are Jewish, Polish, Ukranian, and Italian. Speaking for them at this moment in history is a great responsibility because they have been unrepresented and ignored for so long and their needs are so many and so urgent.

But I hope if I am remembered it will finally be for what I have done, not for what I happen to be. And I hope that my having made it, the hard way, can be some kind of inspiration, particularly to women. The number of women in politics has never been large, but now it is getting even smaller.

Women are a majority of the population, but they are treated like a minority group. The prejudice against them is so widespread that, paradoxically, most persons do not yet realize it exists. Indeed, most women do not realize it. They even accept being paid less for doing the same work as a man. They are as quick as any male to condemn a woman who ventures outside the limits of the role men have assigned to females: that of toy and drudge.

Of my two "handicaps," being female put many more obstacles in my path than being black. Sometimes I have trouble, myself, believing that I made it this far against the odds. No one, not even my father, whose hopes for me were extravagant, would ever have dared to predict it.

Part I
Growing Up

1

Early Years in Barbados

CROP FAILURES caused famines in the Caribbean islands in the early 1920s. Many West Indians fled to the United States, and most of them went to some neighborhood in New York City where they knew a relative or a friend from home was living. As a result, little colonies of islanders grew up all over the city — a Haitian neighborhood in Manhattan, a Trinidadian one on Long Island, and so on.

There was a large colony of Barbadians in Brooklyn, and it was there that my father, Charles St. Hill, and my mother, Ruby Seale, went — separately. He was a native of British Guiana who had grown up in Cuba and Barbados. She was a teen-aged Barbadian girl. They had known each other in Barbados, but not well; in Brooklyn they got better acquainted, fell in love, and married. I was born in 1924. My sister Odessa came about a year later, and two years later my sister Muriel.

Mother was still only a girl herself and had trouble coping with three babies, especially her oldest. I learned to walk and talk very early. By the time I was two and a half, no bigger than a mite (I have never weighed much more than 100 pounds), I was already dominating other children around me — with my mouth. I lectured them and ordered them around. Even Mother was almost afraid of me.

Once, when I was still not yet three, she left me with the two younger girls. "Look out for Dess and Mu," she instructed me. When she came back, I was walking up and down with five-month-old Muriel in my arms. Mother wanted to shout, but she caught herself; she might have frightened me into dropping the baby. First she took Muriel out of my arms. Then she screamed at me.

Mother was a seamstress; she had probably gone to Belmont Market, a five-block-long confusion of pushcarts selling anything that could be loaded on a pushcart, to buy cloth. Her sewing machine fascinated me. I would go to it and turn and turn its wheels. When Mother went out, she tried to put the machine up where I couldn't reach it, but I piled up chairs and climbed until I could.

"It might be a good thing to take her to a farm," Mother began to suggest to Father. "She could run and play there." Mother was thinking of my grandmother's farm in Barbados. Her idea made a lot of sense economically. The middle 1920s may have been a time of legendary prosperity for some Americans, but not enough of it was rubbing off on young black immigrant couples in the big city. My father was unskilled. He worked as a baker's helper and later as a factory hand. His pay, even supplemented by what Mother could earn by sewing, was not much for a family of five. How could they ever save to buy a house and provide educations for their girls?

It is important to notice that they never questioned they had to do these things; Barbadians are like that. They are bright, thrifty, ambitious people. The other islanders call them "Black Jews." One of the smallest islands in the Caribbean, only 133 square miles, Barbados is a rocky place, not lush like Jamaica or Trinidad. Its residents call it Little Scotland. Both its landscape and the character of its citizens make the name apt. Incidentally, my mother's people way back came from Scotland, it was said.

The Barbadians are almost more British than the British and are very proud of their heritage. For instance, they brag that on Barbados the slaves were freed before they were on the other islands. Barbados has the highest literacy rate in the Caribbean — 94 percent. The Barbadians' drive to achieve and excell is almost an obsession and is a characteristic that other islanders do not share to the same degree. The Barbadians who came to Brooklyn all wanted, and most of them got, the same two things: a brownstone house and a college education for their children.

So early in 1928 a diminutive young black woman sailed out of New York Harbor on an old steamer named the *Vulcania* with her three little girls, three, two, and eight months, and ten trunks full of food and clothing bound for Barbados and her mother's farm. She planned to board us there until she and Father had saved enough to assure our future in the States.

The trip took nine days, and the *Vulcania* pitched and swayed terribly on the rough Atlantic all the way to Bridgetown, the capital of Barbados. I still remember arriving: the delays for customs inspection and health clearance, the bus we boarded to ride to the village of Vauxhall where we were going to live, and the dusty, uneven roads past small, pretty houses and through villages where the bus chased chickens and stray animals out of the road.

When the bus stopped, there was Grandmother — Mrs. Emily Seale, a tall, gaunt, erect, Indian-looking woman with her hair knotted on her neck. I did not know it yet, but this stately woman with a stentorian voice was going to be one of the few persons whose authority I would never dare to defy, or even question. There were endless hugs, laughter, tears, and chatter. In less than an hour a truck came with the ten trunks, and Mother had to search through most of them to find our nightclothes. We had our baths in a big galvanized tub in the back yard and were put to bed for our first night in Barbados.

The night noises bothered us city children for a long time: the clucking of chickens hit by cars when they dawdled in the road, the cows mooing and sheep bleating, the crickets, and all the unidentifiable sounds around a farm after dark.

The house was a large frame building with many rooms, most of them bedrooms of various sizes. The parlor was rectangular and furnished mainly with straight-backed bamboo chairs. The kitchen had an old-fashioned coal range and innumerable cast-iron kettles, pots, and frying pans. The toilet was outdoors in the back yard. The furniture was sparse and plain, but we found Grandmother's house elaborately furnished with the two necessities: warmth and love.

Mother stayed for six months to help us get used to this new place, and there were many tears when she had to leave. It must have been much harder for her than for us. She knew she would not see us for several years, although she did not know it would be seven years or that after she was back in Brooklyn a fourth baby would come, another girl whom she and Father would name Selma.

We children had each other, Grandmother, Mother's younger brother Lincoln and younger sister Myrtle, and no fewer than four cousins for company. Mother's older sister Violet was also married and living in the States, and she had come to the same decision Mother and Father had: it would be best for a while if her four children lived at the farm while she helped her young husband earn more and try to save something.

We seven children ranged up to nine years old. There was a lot for us to explore, even though it was a small farm and a small village. The village houses brightly painted white, blue, red, green, or yellow each had a garden in front to grow yams, sweet potatoes, pumpkins, cassava, and breadfruit — mainstays of the Caribbean diet. Each had four or five large rooms, like Grandmother Seale's, and like hers most of them had a small piece of farmland behind the house.

Many of the men went by bus to Bridgetown every day to work. They held unskilled jobs, for the most part. My uncle Lincoln was an exception; he was a writer on the Bridgetown newspaper, a better-paying job than most. Twice a week the women and some of the men went to market, usually on Tuesdays and Saturdays. The women carried their produce on trays balanced on their heads, loads as heavy as seventy-five pounds that they carried several miles in the hot sun. Their posture, as a result, was superb. The village had a small store, a cobbler and a smith, and a church that doubled as a school on weekdays.

On the farm there were goats, pigs, chickens, ducks, sheep, and cows to learn about. And there was the well, a place we got to know too thoroughly; every night for years, it was the children's first chore to draw bucket after bucket from it by hand and carry them to the farm to water the animals, then fill the big galvanized tank next to the house where all the water was stored for drinking, cooking, and washing.

Soon I was four, and Grandmother decided it was time for me to start in the village school. Years later I would know what an important gift my parents had given me by seeing to it that I had my early education in the strict, traditional, British-style schools of Barbados. If I speak and write easily now, that early education is the main reason.

Schooling is important on the islands. Teachers and parents are allied against children. "You are to pay attention to the teacher and learn," children are told sternly. Teachers are free to whip children, and use that freedom liberally. If a child comes home and reports that the teacher hit him, he can expect another beating, probably on his bare bottom. Psychologists now are sure this is bad for children. In my experience, it was not bad for us; I got my share of floggings, and it produced the effect that was desired. I went to school to pay attention and to learn.

The school was a white, wooden building, not large, with one room in which seven classes were separated by blackboards and by the arrangement of benches. When all seven classes were at work, 125 children reading aloud, spelling, reciting history or arithmetic, it was like a Tower of Babel.

In the primer class, I learned to read and write before I was five. Theoretically, my eye and hand muscles were not developed enough at that age. Psychological theories did not get much attention then from educators in the British West Indies. I have always believed that many teachers underestimate the powers of children.

We practiced writing on slates, with slate pencils, and cleaned the slates by spitting on them and wiping them with our hands. Penmanship standards were high, even for the youngest. The levels were, of course, called "forms" and not grades. The curriculum was austere: reading, writing, arithmetic, and history, meaning British history, naturally. The children ranged from four to about eleven. After the sixth form, most of them would go into apprenticeship in some trade like carpentry or shoemaking, or go to work on the family farm. Barbados is an island of small farms. Few would go to college, although there are two good colleges on the island. To go, they would have to take a preparatory course at a private school. To pay for that, some families made the ultimate sacrifice, selling a prized cow or brood sow.

We went to school from eight to four. When we came home, the first thing we had to do was take off our school clothes, which were issued clean on Monday and had to stay that way through Friday. Then we carried the water and helped with the other chores, feeding the chickens and ducks, gathering eggs, changing the straw bedding for the cattle and sheep. The sheep and goats were let out to graze on the abundant grass. There were no fences, so we children had to watch them, to keep them from straying into the road or the gullies, and bring them back at dark.

Four years passed, barefoot, winterless years. Then we moved, from Vauxhall to a place called the Low Rocks, but it was much the same — another farm, another village, and another school. Miss Birch, the headmistress, might have been a caricature of a British schoolmarm. A lanky spinster, she always wore high-necked dresses and high-topped white boots with more than two dozen buttons on each one. Every morning, while we small colonials stood in ranks to sing "God Save the King" and "Rule, Britannia," Miss Birch saw to it that we stood proudly. She stalked quietly behind each line with a little leather whip and punished the slightest hint of a slouch with a vicious lash on the legs.

Always a major part of our lives was the Caribbean, with its warm, blue and aquamarine, incredibly clear water, just a short run from the farm. We stripped and swam and rolled on the sand; the adults swam naked too; there was perfect matter-of-factness about nudity. The most terrible punishment Grandmother could give us was to tell us we couldn't go to the beach. Almost as bad was to be kept home from a market day in the village, where you could snatch oranges or apples from a peddler who wasn't looking.

In Brooklyn, things had not been going the way Mother and Father had planned. The depression had come, and their industry and frugality could not bring the security they had been counting on. But they missed us, Mother especially, who feared that her children would soon be grown and never really come to know her. At the end of 1933, the St. Hills decided that, come what may, it was time to get their family back together.

2

Back to Brooklyn

WHEN MOTHER BROUGHT MURIEL, Odessa, and me back to Brooklyn, it was March 1934. I remember that year that the newspapers were full of pictures and stories about the Dionne quintuplets, who were born a few months after we returned.

All three of us were frightened by the cold. Mother, Father, and Selma were living at 110 Liberty Avenue in Brownsville. It was an unheated, four-room, cold-water railroad flat. Like the cars on a train, the rooms were in a line and you had to go through one to reach the next one. You came into the kitchen, went on through two bedrooms, and arrived at the parlor in the back. But the only heat came from a coal stove in the kitchen and none of it got to the back room, so the parlor was closed and forgotten all winter. Some days when Mother went to Belmont Market we children used to stay in bed most of the day to keep warm. To this day, I'm still afraid of the cold.

Brownsville in the 1930s was a heavily Jewish neighborhood of run-down tenements, some up to ten stories tall with twenty or more apartments. Today we would probably call it a "ghetto." Its residents then would have laughed at the word. Some of them were first-generation Jews from central and eastern Europe, and they knew the difference. They had come from real ghettos.

Most of our playmates and many of Mother's and Father's neighbors were, of course, white and Jewish. Mother's sense of humor appealed to her white friends; they would roar at her imitation of their dialect. The other women often gathered around her bench in the park when she took us there in good weather. Because she was English-speaking and could give advice about bills and other legal pitfalls of city life, she became a kind of neighborhood oracle and leader.

The city was so different from the island, apart from the terrible cold. I kept getting lost. When Mother sent me on short errands, I got mixed up at the corners. Once I had to go to a store about ten blocks away, and she gave me careful written directions. I found my way there and back without trouble, but a few weeks later when I had to go again, I got lost. A store I had relied on as a landmark had moved away. Things didn't change that way in Barbados. The village shoemaker's shop, for example, had been in the same place for generations. I couldn't get used to keeping on the sidewalk, either. When it was crowded I would take to the street, and Mother would scold, "Shirley, you gonna get killed someday."

The movies in Brooklyn were one of our first great discoveries. Mother usually managed to give us each ten cents to go on Saturdays. The screen was so big; we had never seen anything like it in the islands. We stayed through show after show, long past suppertime, sometimes for twelve or thirteen hours, until Mother came for us with a strap. The manager got to know her. "They're up front in the middle, Mrs. St.

Hill," he told her. Mother would herd us home, scolding all the way.

She was thoroughly British in her ideas, her manners and her plans for her daughters. We were to become young ladies — poised, modest, accomplished, educated, and graceful, prepared to take our places in the world. Later Mother and Papa bought a piano, a luxury they could not afford even though it was only twenty-five dollars and was not in the best repair. I went to piano lessons for nine years. When I began to show progress, they made an even greater sacrifice; they bought a new piano on time.

My father was working then as a helper in a big cake bakery. I idolized him, his good looks, his extensive vocabulary, and his intelligence. A tall, thin, handsome man with white hair (it turned in his early twenties), brown skin, and a straight, Grecian nose, he would have been a brilliant scholar if he had been able to go to college. He was an omnivorous reader. Even during the depression, he always bought two or three newspapers a day. Mother never understood his spending the money; she thought he could get all the news from one. Papa read everything within reach. If he saw a man passing out handbills, he would cross the street to get one and read it. The result was that, although he only finished the equivalent of fifth grade, he seemed to know a little about almost everything.

A tireless talker, he had dozens of friends whom he brought home in the evenings for the sake of their conversation. Papa never smoked or drank, but he kept whiskey for his friends. Mother scolded over that. "That's all they come for, Charles, you know you can't afford to entertain the way you want to. And you never know when to tell them to go." Mother was upset, not only at the cost of the whiskey with which Papa was so liberal, but also at the fact that we girls had to undress and go to bed in the next room while the men sat around the table in the kitchen. Lying in bed, we could hear them talk about the islands and their politics. Papa and his friends traded story after story showing how Britain was oppressing the colonial peoples of the world. He would speak scornfully of "the divine right of kings."

Papa was a Garveyite, too, a follower of Marcus Garvey, the Jamaican who originated many of the ideas that characterize today's militant black separatists. Garvey used to write and speak against "the mulatto leader," W. E. B. Du Bois, and the "light element of Negroes" — his phrase for the National Association for the Advancement of Colored People — who, he said, believed in miscegenation and an end to the race problem through racial mixing. Garvey declared in the 1920s that "black is beautiful" and called on blacks to preserve their racial purity by becoming separate. His goal was to unite American blacks and return them to Africa, where they would become the equals of any man, in independent isolation. I think this appealed to my father because he, too, was a very proud black man. He instilled pride in his children, a pride in ourselves and our race that was not as fashionable at that time as it is today.

Much of the kitchen-table talk had to do with unions. Papa belonged to the Confectionery and Bakers International Union, and there was nothing he was more proud of than being a union man. He brought labor newspapers home and read from them to his friends. When he was elected a shop steward at the bakery, you would have thought he had been made a king. He had to have his shoes shined and wear a tie when he went to union meetings. It was the first time in his life he had been given the recognition his talents deserved.

Dinner together every night was an inflexible rule in our family. The table had to be set when Papa got there. We waited for him to say a blessing before anything was passed. Then he would lead the conversation, telling Mother about the events of his day and asking the children the inevitable question, "What did you learn in school?" It was no idle query; he wanted an answer. Papa harped on the theme, "You must make something of yourselves. You've got to go to school, and I'm not sending you to play either. Study and make something of yourselves. Remember, only the strong people survive in this world. God gave you a brain; use it."

Sometimes Papa would hold forth on his idol — hardly too strong a word — Marcus Garvey. He seemed almost to worship Garvey and was particularly proud of the fact he was a West Indian, too. Papa believed America had treated Garvey wrongly, and as a result he talked negatively about the country. "America's got a lot to learn," Papa often proclaimed. When any organization had a Marcus Garvey tribute, he would dress up and go. Sometimes he took me, and there I heard my first black nationalist oratory — talk of race pride and the need for unity, despite any differences, because, the speakers stressed, "We have a common enemy."

My aunt Violet and her husband, Clement Jones, lived about fifteen minutes away. Aunt Violet and her four children had come back to Brooklyn with Mother and her girls, and we usually visited each other on weekends. On Saturdays, these two poor women would sometimes pack lunches and take their combined broods of seven active children by bus or train to Jones Beach, Coney Island, or some other spot for a picnic. Papa seldom went; he usually had to work on Saturdays.

School had been a setback for me at first. When we left Barbados, I had just been promoted to the sixth form, so I expected to be put in the sixth grade in Brooklyn. At P.S. 84 on Glenmore Avenue, the teachers were satisfied with my reading and writing ability, but horrified by my ignorance of American history and geography. They put me in grade 3-B, with children two years younger than I was. Bored, I became a discipline problem. I carried rubber bands in the pocket of my middy blouse and snapped them at the other children; I became expert at making spitballs and flicking them when the teacher's back was turned. Luckily someone diagnosed the trouble and did something about it. The school provided me with a tutor in American geography and history for a year and a half, until I caught up with and passed my age-grade level.

My sisters and I and the other black children were a minority at P.S. 84, but we were not much concerned about it. Blacks from the islands and the growing number from the South would in a few years reverse the racial make-up of the neighborhood and the change would be accompanied by mounting bad feeling, but at that time the race line was not drawn in the same way it is today. As I remember it, the school was about 80 percent white, mostly Jewish children; all the teachers were white, and nearly all were Jewish. We were not particularly conscious of that fact, either.

On Saturdays, my sisters and I often sat on our fire escape and giggled at the Jewish neighbors going in and out of the synagogue. Mother punished us when she caught us at it. She was a deeply religious person, and would not hear of our making fun of anyone's religion. Other children made fun of us because Mother enforced churchgoing on her daughters — three times every Sunday. They would chant, "Here come the St. Hill girls!" as Mother, Odessa, Muriel, Selma, and I, dressed up and each carrying a little Bible, walked to 11:00 A.M. services, 2:30 P.M. Bible service, and 7:30 P.M. services at the English Brethren Church. It was a small, Quaker-like sect that Mother belonged to. "You're going to grow up to be good Christians," she would tell us firmly, leading us past our playmates' jeers.

There was no formal service and no minister at the Brethren church. Benches were arranged in concentric circles in a large, bare room. Like a Quaker meeting, the service consisted largely of long silences. What we girls hated most was that we could never even whisper. A head brother would lead the congregation in an opening hymn, a cappella, because instruments were worldly and taboo. Then there would be silence until someone was moved by the spirit to preach or pray. When he was through there were amens, and then more silence. In the middle, the head brother would lead another hymn. It was an hour and ten minutes of this morning and evening, with Bible study in the afternoon.

"The St. Hill girls" used to have to endure a lot of ridicule for the old-world way their parents controlled their lives. We were always the first ones to arrive at a party and the first to leave. If a party was at eight, we were there one minute early, in beautiful party dresses. However poor we were, Mother could always buy remnants at the market and make us dresses. Always, just as the party got going and I was starting to enjoy dancing, Odessa would come up with the self-righteous air of a girl who has a chance to tell her older sister what to do. "You remember what Mummy said. We've been here an hour and it's time to go home."

Whenever we left the house, Mother and Father always had a long list of dos and don'ts. As we got older, naturally we began to rebel. Our friends seemed to be having so much more fun. Our parents were too old-fashioned. They didn't give us any freedom at all.

About 1936, we moved to 420 Ralph Avenue in Bedford-Stuyvesant. Their girls were getting bigger, and Mother and Father needed more room. The new apartment had only four

rooms, too, but they were bigger and it was steam heated.
It was over a candy store. The proprietor, our landlord, lived
in back of the store downstairs and another black family lived
upstairs.

"Bed-Stuy" was about 50 percent black in those days. After
we moved there, I began to hear racial slurs and epithets for
the first time — nigger, kike, Jew bastard, black son of a
bitch. I was not used to black being used as a derogatory
word.

Blacks were arriving in greater numbers from the South.
But though their numbers were growing, there was no such
thing as a black community. Most of the newcomers were passive and accommodating in the face of discrimination. They
knew their place and stayed in it. They talked among themselves, but there was no racial consciousness, no leadership.

I finished grade school at P.S. 28, and then went to J.H.S.
178, which is still there. It is one of the schools in the Ocean
Hill–Brownsville unit that is fighting to stay alive as an independent, locally controlled, and community-responsive school
complex.

Those were the hardest years of the depression. Dad had
changed jobs and was working as a laborer in a burlap bag
factory. He had expected to gain several dollars a week by
the move, but it turned out that the work was not steady.
Soon he was working as little as two days a week and bringing
home sometimes no more than eighteen dollars. Mother had
to do something she had always feared. She put a key on a
string around my neck and went to work as a domestic for
white families in Flatbush. Every noon I had to walk from
junior high school to P.S. 28 and collect my sisters, take them
home and feed them, and return them to school. I was usually late getting back, but the teachers knew why and made
allowances. Lunch was usually a glass of milk and a bun.

Every Thursday Mother gave me a quarter to go to a bakery and buy whatever was marked down as stale — bread, cake, or pie, enough for the week. She told us to go straight home at the end of the day, lock the door, and not open it for anyone until she got home. We sat in the front window, watching for the first glimpse of her. When she came in sight we always screamed out in excitement, and the landlord downstairs would always shout, "Shut up!"

Papa's new job was a lot better, and when he worked he came home at night exhausted. His hands were rough and callused from the tons of rough burlap he carried, and when he tried to read in the evening he fell asleep over his book.

We had to read, too, even if we did not want to. We all had library cards and every other Saturday Mother took us to the library to check out the limit, three books each. Each of us had a dictionary, and our Christmas presents were books, often one of those endless "adventure" series such as the Nancy Drew or Bobbsey Twins stories.

When I graduated from junior high school in 1939 I went to Girls' High School, one of Brooklyn's oldest schools, on Nostrand Avenue in Bedford-Stuyvesant. We had moved again while I was in high school — to 316 Patchen Avenue, where my father worked as the janitor so we had a six-room apartment free, and Mother could stay home again — and it was only a short walk to school. Many of the other students walked or rode there from the farthest parts of Brooklyn. The school was highly regarded. As the name indicates, it was all girls; about half of them were white, but the neighborhood by now was nearly all black.

Immigrants from the South were streaming to Brooklyn for jobs at the Brooklyn Navy Yard, the Long Island aircraft plants, and other growing defense industries. No one knew it then, but the present-day "inner city" (to use a white euphemism) was being created. Black workers had to crowd into neighborhoods that were already black or partly so, because they could not find homes anywhere else. Buildings that had four apartments suddenly had eight, and bathrooms that had been private were shared. White building inspectors winked at housing code violations and illegal rates of occupancy, white landlords doubled and trebled their incomes on slum buildings, and the white neighborhoods in other parts of town and in the suburbs stayed white. Today's urban ghettos were being born.

My family still kept me on a tight rein in my high school years. Mother knew to the minute when I should get home from school, and I had to be there on the dot or face a barrage of questions. My father remonstrated with Mother sometimes: "Ruby, you must remember these are American kids, not island kids. You are here in America." Mother was not impressed. We girls were allowed to go to school programs and occasional parties, but I never had a date, a regular date, in high school. In fact, I never had one in college.

The blessing of a high IQ combined with my good study habits (Mother and Father would not have stood for any other kind) to keep me in the upper percentiles at school. I won a French medal; at a time when black students were seldom elected to offices, I was vice president of a girls' honor society, Junior Arista.

Frustration grew, naturally, as I saw my friends doing things I was forbidden to do. My rebellion took small forms. I began to play popular songs on the piano and started trying to play jazz by ear. When boys walked me home, I had them bring me to the door instead of leaving me on the corner. One night Mother opened the door and discovered me being kissed. She dragged me inside while the boy fled, and began to lecture me: "I don't want you to carry on in the streets.

Bring your friends home." But when I did, I was embarrassed. They had to leave by ten o'clock, and if they didn't, Mother took direct action. She came in the parlor in her nightgown and started pulling down the shades.

Mother always took the lead in handling social relationships, and Papa let her do so, perhaps because we were all girls. If we had been boys, perhaps he would have taken a greater hand. He felt sorry for us, I know, but he never intervened. Sometimes he would lecture Mother, trying to persuade her that she was an immigrant and should adapt more to the ways of her new country instead of trying to transplant all the values of the islands. Mother would not listen. "Charles," she would respond, "we've got to be strict on them if we want them to grow up to be something."

When I graduated from Girls High in 1942 I drew several scholarship offers. I wanted to accept either one from Vassar or one from Oberlin. But my parents argued that they could not afford my room and board at an out-of-town school. I had to admit they were right, and in the fall I went to Brooklyn College.

3

College Years

IF I HAD GONE TO VASSAR, the rest of my life might have been different. Would I have become one of the pseudo-white upper-middle-class black women professionals, or a doctor's wife with furs, limousines, clubs, and airs? I can't believe that would have happened, but one never knows. At any rate, Brooklyn College changed my life. I was still naive about most things when I entered college, not quite eighteen. My fiercely protective parents had given me a sheltered upbringing that was incredible, considering the time and place in which I grew up. In school, my intelligence had put me in a special category. In college, I began to bump up against more of the world.

One needed an 89 percent average to enter Brooklyn College then, so there were only about sixty black students in the day school. Brooklyn was the largest of the five city-run colleges, and its campus was supposed to be especially for bright lower-class, poorer students. Tuition was free; it was a "subway campus," and one would have expected more black students. The trouble was, of course, that the grade and high schools they attended — then as now — did not do enough to overcome the handicaps of their background. So 98 percent of the students at the city colleges were white.

Brooklyn College was alive with activity. Bulletin boards and walls were full of posters for meetings, clubs, and programs. There were more organizations and extracurricular activities than anyone could count. Many of them were politically oriented and most of these were ultraprogressive. Brooklyn's president, Dr. Harry Gideonse, was always under attack from some office seeker who claimed that the faculty was riddled with Reds. It wasn't, of course, but for those days it was radical.

I had already decided to become a teacher. There was no other road open to a young black woman. Law, medicine, even nursing were too expensive, and few schools would admit black men, much less a woman. Social work was not yet open to blacks in the early 1940s. If I had other ideas about what I might do, I dismissed them. My youth may have been sheltered from boys and some other realities, but I was black, and nobody needed to draw me a diagram. No matter how well I prepared myself, society wasn't going to give me a chance to do much of anything else. (My sister Muriel, who entered Brooklyn College a few years later, majored in physics and graduated magna cum laude. She was unable to find a job, even as a laboratory technician.) I knew it would have to be teaching for me; but I took no education courses, for some reason. I majored in sociology and minored in Spanish.

There was one all-black student group, the Harriet Tubman Society. Some upperclassmen had started it, about a year before I joined it in my sophomore year. There I first heard people other than my father talk about white oppression, black racial consciousness, and black pride. The black students kept to their own tables in the cafeteria. We talked.

No one said "rap" then, but that's what we did. I had some things to contribute, more out of my reading than my experience. I knew about Harriet Tubman and Frederick Douglass, W. E. B. Du Bois and George W. Carver, and I had managed to find some books in the public library about our African heritage that few people then studied or talked about; I knew about the Ashanti kingdoms, for instance. Some of the Tubman Society speakers warned of the future: "The day is going to come when blacks and whites will be at each other's throats in their own communities." We found that hard to believe then, although the 1943 Detroit riots had happened to serve as a portent.

Other experiences sharpened my feeling for how racism was woven through American life. I belonged to the Political Science Society, which naturally thought itself progressive. Some of its speakers, I became aware, looked at my people as another breed, less human than they. Politicians came to talk and gave us such liberal sentiments as, "We've got to help the Negro because the Negro is limited," or, "Of course, the Negro people have always been the laborers and will continue to be. So we've got to make it more comfortable for them." Few white speakers would dare to say such things even to all-white audiences now. They were more innocent about prejudice twenty years ago.

For a long time I watched such white people closely, listened to them, and observed silently the treatment blacks were given in social and political situations. It grew on me that we, black men especially, were expected to be subservient even in groups where ostensibly everyone was equal. Blacks played by those rules; if a white man walked in, they came subtly to attention. But I could see their fear, helplessness, and discomfort.

When I looked at the white people who were doing this, consciously or not, it made me angry because so many of them were baser, less intelligent, less talented than the people they were lording it over. But the whites were in control. We could do nothing about it. We had no power. That was the way society was. I perceived that this was the way it was meant to be: things were organized to keep those who were on top up there. The country was racist all the way through.

More and more people, white and black, began to tell me things like, "Shirley, you have potential. You should do something with your life." I felt they were right. There must be a role for me to play, but what? As a teacher, perhaps I could use the talents people were telling me about and which I felt were there to do something that would be of service to society — especially to children. I volunteered to work in an Urban League settlement house, teaching art classes and sewing, and writing and producing skits and plays, which I loved. I decided to devote my life to children. But the resolve was also there (I did not realize yet how fierce it had grown) to do something about the way whites treated my people. Political action was hardly even a fantasy for me at that time. But I decided that if I ever had a chance, somehow I would tell the world how things were as I saw them.

A blind political science professor, Louis Warsoff, became interested in me, and we had long talks. I called him "Proffy," affectionately. He was one of the first white men whom I ever really knew and trusted. Our white neighbors and my father's co-workers had never been friends; they did not visit us and we did not visit them, and our interrelations were always a little strained even when they were at their best. From Professor Warsoff I learned that white people were not really different from me. I loved formal debating particularly, and once after I starred in a match he told me, "You ought to go into politics." I was astonished at his naiveté.

"Proffy," I said, "you forget two things. I'm black — and I'm a woman."

"You really have deep feelings about that, haven't you?" he countered. The conversation stuck in my mind. I realized that I did have deep feelings, on both scores.

Women were not even elected to campus offices then. Twice when girls ran for president of the Student Council (they were white, of course) I threw myself into the campaigns. I painted posters, helped write slogans and speeches, helped organize rallies and spoke at them myself. The white girls did not win.

Black students were not welcome in social clubs, so some friends and I formed a sororitylike black women students' society that I named Ipothia, which stood for "in pursuit of the highest in all." We were tired of trying to get into white groups, and decided, "Who needs them?" Ipothia grew to about twenty-six members. It is gone now; white groups started taking in black students, and the need for Ipothia passed.

I was still living at home, still going to church three times on Sundays, and still forbidden to date. I spent hours in the college library, and made no new, close friends in school. Naturally, the boys considered me a bookworm. It didn't bother me too much. They were surprised, though, when I showed up at parties and they discovered that I could dance, and loved to. No one ever had to teach me how; I just naturally danced. "That Shirley St. Hill can really move on the floor," I heard one boy say. But still the word was "Stay away from her — she's too intellectual, always talking about some big, serious thing."

During college I joined the Brooklyn chapter of the NAACP, but I was not too active. It was primarily interested in economic issues such as discrimination in hiring, working conditions, pay, promotion. I had begun what was to be a twenty-year-long round of involvement with one community service organization after another, most of which I would eventually drop. I worked for the Urban League, I worked in hospitals, reading to old people and organizing programs to entertain them. I am still active in a few of these groups, like the Brooklyn Home for the Aged. As for the rest, after I give an organization a fair chance to show that it is really out to do something, if it doesn't, I get angry. In the last twenty years I have sat through more meetings and discussions than I ever want to remember and have seen very little get done. Even as an undergraduate, I was beginning to feel how useless it was for blacks to sit and talk with "the leading people" in the community, on biracial committees. It had begun to be clear that as long as we kept talking, nothing much was going to happen, and that this was what the "leading people" really wanted.

During 1945 we moved for the last time, when my father bought a house, a solid three-story one on Prospect Place. It cost him $10,000, all of it painfully saved from his wages at the bag factory, where he worked until his death. My mother and two of my sisters still live there; Selma, who is unmarried, lives on the second floor, and Odessa has her own apartment with her husband and her two children. Buying a house had always been my parents' second great goal; an education for their children was the only thing that mattered more to them. Now they had provided for both, which was a really remarkable achievement for parents of four children, who started with nothing and lived through the depression on a laborer's and a domestic's pay.

When I graduated in 1946, cum laude, I was nearly twenty-two but I looked sixteen or seventeen; I weighed about ninety pounds. It made job hunting hard. School after school turned me down, even as a teacher's aide; I didn't look old enough to teach, and most of my interviewers told me so. Day after day I stomped the streets. Finally I blew up at one nursery school director. "At least you could try me!" I exploded. "Put me on as a probationer! Give me a chance to show you! Give me a chance to find out whether I can do the job . . . don't judge me by my size." Mrs. Eula Hodges, director of the Mt. Calvary Child Care Center in Harlem, was persuaded. I worked there for seven years.

Even before I had finished my probation and become a full-fledged teacher's aide, I was sure that this was going to be my lifework. So, to be as well prepared as possible, I enrolled in Columbia University to work evenings for a master's degree in early childhood education. It was about then that I had my own early education in politics, in the toughest and most instructive school possible, New York City's old-time clubhouses.

4

Starting in Politics

THE POLITICAL CLUBS are still there in New York, but things ain't what they used to be for the clubhouse crowds, and I hope they never are again. The clubs had legitimate functions, but most of them are now being taken over by newer organizations. Legal services, for example. The clubhouse lawyers used to advise poor people in exchange for an express or implied pledge of their voting regularity. Now nobody needs them. In the same way, there are newer and less predatory agencies to lend a hand to people with housing, welfare, or employment problems.

New York's clubs were organized by state Assembly districts. Often the assemblyman was also the district leader and state committeeman. Both parties had clubs, but in most parts of the city "club" meant the Democratic club. Once a month the club had a membership meeting, but the important meetings were the "club nights" on Monday and Thursday evenings. Those were the nights people came in with their problems. In the old Seventeenth Assembly District Democratic Club, the leader, Vincent Carney, used to sit with his flunkies on a dais at the far end of the room, while the

voters came in and took high-backed chairs to wait their turns
for an audience.

The blacks sat at one side, the whites on the other. There
was no sign that said "Colored Side." It was an unwritten
law. In many of the clubs even in the 1940s blacks were not
welcome, unless they were brought in by a white member.
In the 17th A.D. Club, they came but they stayed in their
place. You could feel the men on each side daring those on
the other to cross the invisible line. The blacks did not go to
club nights because they felt wanted, or because they hoped
to make any real inroads in the organization. They went
because they needed help.

The 17th A.D. at that time was probably two-thirds black,
but the all-white (mostly Irish) organization ran the district.
It elected the state senator, assemblyman, city councilman,
and other local officeholders and, by treaty with the similar
clubs around it, picked the men for congressional seats, judge-
ships, and other big-bore political jobs.

During college, I had gone to a few club meetings when
there was a speaker I wanted to hear. After the city councilman or commissioner had finished, there was a question
period. But hardly anyone ever asked questions. I did. I
asked the sanitation commissioner why trash wasn't picked up
regularly in Bedford-Stuyvesant, as it was in white neighborhoods. I asked councilmen why they hadn't delivered on
their promises. Such questions were unwelcome, and after
the meeting someone was likely to tell me so. I pretended
innocence: How do I know what kind of questions you're
supposed to ask? But I knew very well, and so did they, that
I was needling them to show how little they did or cared for
the people who kept them in office.

One night I tried another challenge. I walked in the room
and right past the rows of people waiting, black on one side

and white on the other, and up on the dais. Two men blocked my way and told me I wasn't waiting my turn; I would have to go back to the end of the line and take a chair. I told them, "No. This is an urgent matter." I don't even remember now what it was, something for somebody else. I just wanted to see what they would do. I had been watching people sit and wait, evening after evening, and it had grown on me. It was insulting and degrading to them; they were being treated like cattle. Why should they have to sit there on hard, high-backed chairs, stiff, formal, and uncomfortable? They made an exception and talked to me. It didn't change the system though.

During my senior year in college, my hairdresser, Mrs. Cleo Skeete, did something that changed my life. "I know a man you really ought to know," she told me one day, and she introduced me to Wesley McD. Holder. I had heard of him: a black man from Guiana who had been upsetting white politicians as far back as the 1930s. Mac, a former editor of the *Amsterdam News,* had worked in Washington, but came home to New York to work for an idea that was ahead of its time. He was out to elect black candidates to represent black communities. Mac was and still is, in his seventies, the shrewdest, toughest, and hardest-working black political animal in Brooklyn, probably in New York City, and maybe elsewhere. He is manager of my district congressional office now, but that is getting a long way ahead of the story.

The black community had less sense of brotherhood in those days, and, worse yet, black people were almost all afraid. They feared, and justly, the power the white man had over their lives. "The Man will get you," they would warn. "You can't win." The few black people who had jobs through city appointments were the worst of all. If they showed the slightest sign of opposing the system, they were warned, sometimes subtly and sometimes overtly, "Don't bite the hand that's feeding you." Many black men who could have become leaders were neutralized that way. Their jobs were the most important things to them; they held on to what they had. I didn't have that worry. I had my job as a nursery school teacher and I had no family to support. Nobody could touch me.

By the later 1940s, the black community was slowly beginning to catch up to Mac's ideas. It was starting to realize that the organization never had and never would pick black candidates even if the area became 99 percent black, so black citizens would have to organize and fight for candidates of their own. The white power brokers were holding on to everything for themselves, throwing out just a few morsels — never even one important job to make the community feel that black people, too, were competent. They weren't even putting a black man by the front door in those days.

In his time Wesley McD. Holder must have supported nearly everybody in Brooklyn politics and opposed nearly everybody. He has never been elected to public office, but he has left his mark. In 1948, when major Brooklyn hotels still barred black groups, Mac persuaded the Towers Hotel to cater a Phi Beta Sigma fraternity dance. It was the first such color line break in the borough. A few years later, Mac was one of a group that needled city hall over the lack of black representation in government until a Negro, Clarence Wilson, was appointed as a magistrate in Brooklyn. But there were still no black elected officials from Kings County, on the state, city, or national levels.

My interest in politics grew gradually. I joined the Seventeenth Assembly District Democratic Club and scored my first political success there as a cigar box decorator.

When I began going to membership meetings regularly,

they put me on the card party committee. The party and raffle formed the year's big fund-raising event. They were run by the women of the club, most of them wives of members. Because I had a flair for painting and decorating, I was given as my first assignment the job of decorating cigar boxes to hold raffle tickets and money collected at each table during the evening. I went around and begged boxes from candy stores, painted them, and cut out pictures to decorate them. They were so beautiful that all the women were impressed. Definitely, I was going to be an asset to the club. From now on, they would have somebody to collect cigar boxes and decorate them.

When the committee met to discuss the progress of the raffle ticket sales and so on, I went a little beyond the role they had assigned me and began to make suggestions. One turned out to be a real troublemaker.

The club, I could see if they couldn't, was exploiting the women. It lived on the proceeds of the annual raffle and card party that the women ran; its only other income was from dues. But the men never provided a budget to run the event, and the women had to beg money here and there to buy prizes and print raffle books.

"Why should we put up with it?" I asked them. "We bring in the money. Why shouldn't they give us five hundred dollars or a thousand, some definite sum, to do it with?" I was angry, and as we talked, some of the women got angry themselves. They brought it up at a club meeting.

One, Molly, was the spokesman. As one of the male leaders, up front, was blathering compliments at the women for their efforts, Molly stood up and said, "I don't want to hear any of that. I want to hear what you're going to give us this year to run the party." She persisted, and others joined in. The men huddled to see how they were going to handle the crisis. Molly wouldn't quit. "All I want to know is how much you're going to give us." I joined in: "Women are the backbone of this club, and you know it. You gentlemen are always using us. Well, we have no objection to that, as long as you support our efforts and give us some recognition."

The chairman rapped the gavel. "This meeting is out of order." A woman in the back said, "It will stay out of order until you start to pay attention to us." So at last, they gave us $700. The party, as it always did, brought in more than $8000.

After that the women occasionally spoke up at meetings and raised questions. The reaction of the men became "Shirley is egging them on." Sometimes that was true. But I was not really there to make trouble; I thought I was trying to help. The women, who had decided I was worth cultivating, praised me to the men, and this helped a lot; most of them were the wives of officeholders or other party faithfuls. In their minds, of course, I was going to be their "good black woman in the club," a sort of show dog. This was not what I had in mind.

In 1953 Mac Holder formed a group he called the Committee for the Election of Lewis S. Flagg, Jr. Flagg, an outstanding black lawyer, was running for the district's seat on the municipal court bench. When the vacancy had occurred, the machine had gone one step too far. Not only had they passed over the qualified black nominees in the district, they also had imported a white man to run for the job. It outraged many of the blacks and some of the whites. At that time there were forty-nine civil judges in Brooklyn, not one of them black, as Mac pointed out in his campaign mailings. Mac lined up heavy support among the community's big names, black and white. Those of us in the ranks worked overtime canvassing and selling our candidate.

We succeeded. Flagg was elected the first black judge in Brooklyn's history. At the campaign dinner, Mac was in Valhalla. He made an emotional speech saying that he intended to live to see a black city councilman, a black assemblyman and a black congressman representing Bedford-Stuyvesant.

He did more than talk. He tried to hold the Flagg Committee together by turning it into the Bedford-Stuyvesant Political League. The BSPL was, in effect, an insurgent political club. I was in it from the start and gradually became Mac's protégée and one of his chief lieutenants.

The BSPL never repeated its success with Judge Flagg, although it kept trying. In 1954 we ran a full slate against the regular Democrats — black candidates for congressman, state senator, district leader (that was Mac), co-leader and assemblyman. "Make history again!" our pamphlets urged. "The Bedford-Stuyvesant Political League demands fuller and fairer political representation for Negroes. It supports vigorous, militant Negro leadership!"

One trouble was that we weren't the only fish in the pond. Besides the regular Democratic organization, there were other insurgents who came and went. Most black Democrats supported the machine as faithfully as the whites in the primaries. Several black candidates usually split the vote, and the machine's man won. There were Republican candidates, of course, and sometimes Liberals, but they never had a chance. Whoever won the Democratic primary won the district. Most of New York City was like that then. Much of it still is.

But each time the organization slipped a little, and its bosses began to face the fact that someday they might no longer be on top. People were beginning to see that it was their community, and they didn't need a white organization with white councilmen and assemblymen to represent them.

Mac must have tried just about everything in the next eight or ten years. He ran several times against Assemblyman Bertram L. Baker, the only black assemblyman from Brooklyn. He ran against state Senator Walter E. Cooke, but the state supreme court threw his nominating petition out because of what the justice said were "wholesale frauds and irregularities." This is one of the standard techniques that the old Brooklyn machine used to kill off insurgents when everything else had failed. The election laws are designed to make it easy for the men in power. They make the rules and they enforce them. Anybody who plays their game has to play with their deck.

Even though I was active in the BSPL, I stayed in the regular Democratic club. Their treatment of me was interesting. They started with the politician's classic method for handling potential troublemakers. They made me part of the in-group. In their minds, that had to be what I wanted. I was elected to the board of directors, still in my twenties, black, and, worst of all, a woman. Next I found myself elevated to third vice president. The trouble was that I didn't behave.

I was still working with community groups such as the NAACP as well as teaching days and going to Columbia several nights a week. In the service organizations I worked with, we tried to solve some of the myriads of problems that were not being tackled, or even noticed, by the politicians. So I kept bringing questions back to the club meetings, and began to harass the speakers systematically. At membership meetings I would bring up matters that had been discussed at directors' meetings but not disposed of to my satisfaction. Some of the members had been waiting for someone to ask these questions, but they gave me very little overt support.

Presently I got a letter thanking me for my service on the board and saying I was not a member anymore. It was supposed to crush me, I guess, and either bring me into line or get me out of the way. It did neither. I had never asked to be on the board, and I knew why they had put me on it. I went to the next club meeting as usual. Someone asked, "Shirley, you're back with us?" I waved at the dais where the directors sat. "I don't fit in up there."

The experience contained lessons that were valuable over and over. Political organizations are formed to keep the powerful in power. Their first rule is "Don't rock the boat." If someone makes trouble and you can get him, do it. If you can't get him, bring him in. Give him some of the action, let him have a taste of power. Power is all anyone wants, and if he has a promise of it as a reward for being good, he'll be good. Anyone who does not play by those rules is incomprehensible to most politicians.

I was well on the way to forming my present attitude toward politics as it is practiced in the United States: it is a beautiful fraud that has been imposed on the people for years, whose practitioners exchange gilded promises for the most valuable thing their victims own, their votes. And who benefits most? The lawyers. This is true on any level, but at the district politics plane one sees it clearest. There are a few menial jobs for the doorbell ringers, the envelope stuffers, the petition carriers, and the car pool drivers who make the machine go. Some of them get to be charwomen in government buildings, or process servers, or guards. But without a legal background, the real patronage is out of their reach.

The people are beginning to see through the cheat now. The ones in party work wised up first. They delivered the vote, and then some lawyer, with his shirt and tie, too proud to tramp up and down tenement stairs, got the gravy. That's why black people are apt to laugh when one talks about patronage.

The clubs used to welcome immigrants and show them around, including where to register when they became qualified, and how to vote. They gave out turkeys at Thanksgiving and baskets at Christmas. If you were having trouble with a city department, you could go in on Monday or Thursday night and get help. Dispense a favor, create an obligation — the formula worked for years. But new organizations with no political axes to grind are making the machines unnecessary. Some of them are government financed, chiefly by the Office of Economic Opportunity, but the best ones are coming up from the bottom, like the Reverend Jesse Jackson's Operation Breadbasket in Chicago.

Of course, the black community had little part in the old clubs. Blacks had no claim to power. Even if there were a large number in a district, an overwhelming majority, there was never any effort to include them in the party structure. Oh, there was tokenism, a couple of black faces; but the black community was wise. It knew it had no part of the pie, only a few crumbs that were allowed to fall its way.

But even though I kept going to Democratic club meetings and irritating Carney and his crew by asking questions such as "Why can't Bedford-Stuyvesant have as much police protection as other parts of the city?" and "Why aren't the housing codes enforced?" I gradually became less active in the club. The NAACP, the League of Women Voters, the Stuyvesant Community Center, and, most of all, the Bedford-Stuyvesant Political League were taking too much of my time to leave any to waste on them. I was reaching positions of leadership in several of the groups and had become sort of a little local figure.

Mac and the BSPL were pushing voter registration. He intrigued for organization support for a black city councilman, and thought he had it won for himself in 1957 in exchange for his support of a white city court judge who was running for reelection. A black candidate was nominated and elected, but Mac thought he had been double-crossed because he was not the nominee. The next year he started organizing months before the primary to beat the man he blamed, Assemblyman Bertram Baker.

In 1958, Mac and I had a falling-out that lasted for almost ten years. I had become vice president of the League, and was so active — leading delegations to city hall, speaking at rallies — that some of the members began to prod me to go all the way and become president of the League.

At first I held back. Then I agreed. Mac was furious. No one else had ever dared to challenge him. He told me I was being used. I told him there was nothing in the League's constitution that said he was supposed to be president for life. He started telling people I had turned on him. Nowadays he sometimes says, "I made her." There's a lot of truth in that. I learned politics from him. He would explain to me what was happening in politics, what maneuvers the white politicians were making and what they meant, how the deals were being made. I absorbed his sophistication on how the system works, how some people are kept out and others kept in.

So the battle was on, and it was no holds barred. I expected to lose, but I felt stubbornly that I had a right to run. That was what democracy was all about.

Mac was a member of the Mount Lowry Zion Baptist Church, and he had helped it raise hundreds of dollars. He called on the minister, and when the night came for the League election, in the old Paragon Hall on Fulton Street, he was ready. I had told my people to get there early, that we had the votes if we got our seats. The meeting was jammed. A young woman was taking on McD. Holder, whom nobody had ever tackled before. It promised to be a show.

It was. The first thing we found was three sheets of pink paper circulating, full of propaganda for Mac and against me. He had written it himself, with vitriol for ink, and it was such a masterful job of character assassination that it is still famous in the neighborhood. "For three years I've pushed Shirley Chisholm forward," it said. "Tonight she is trying, as a reward, to push me — out." He took credit for my election as a director of the Democratic club and a board member of the Stuyvesant Community Center. There was more, including the "secret" that I had never been elected president of the National Association of College Women's Brooklyn chapter and "these women . . . know her better than some of us."

Then about ten o'clock we began to notice Mac's people were arriving — followed by one after another of the nice old ladies from the Zion Baptist Church. Mac had a table set up at the door, and as each of the sisters came in, one of his representatives was making her out a membership card. When I made my speech, as some of the church ladies told me afterward, they realized that they hadn't known the whole story, and a few of them voted for me. But I lost.

That was the end of Mac's and my political alliance for the time being. The League itself lasted only a few years more; the fight had split and weakened Mac's effectiveness as a leader. None of its candidates succeeded as Judge Flagg had. The regular Democrats, black voters and white, were still supporting the machine in the primaries. For the time being, I was not in the struggle.

Part II
Getting There

5

Teaching, Marriage, and the Political Arena

WHEN I LEFT the Bedford-Stuyvesant Political League, in 1958, I had nowhere to go politically. That suited me; I was becoming more and more absorbed in my profession, and several things had happened in my personal life, including marriage.

At the Mt. Calvary Child Care Center, I had become a teacher, not a teacher's aide. In 1953 I became director of a private nursery school, the Friend in Need Nursery, on Bradford Street near Atlantic Avenue in Brooklyn. After one year there, I was offered the directorship of the large Hamilton-Madison Child Care Center in Manhattan, at 60 Catherine Street, within sight of city hall. I went there in 1954 and stayed until 1959, supervising a staff of twenty-four teachers and maintenance personnel who cared for the physical, social, emotional, and intellectual needs of 130 youngsters between the ages of three and seven.

The first man in my life had entered the picture late in my last year at Brooklyn College. During Easter vacation, I found a job in a jewelry factory in Manhattan, and rode the subway to work every day, carrying my lunch, under strict orders from Mother to eat by myself and not mingle with the other employees. I obeyed, but on the third day a handsome, older man whom I had noticed watching me came over. He began kidding me about eating alone and exerted all his charm (which was enormous). The next day and every day after that I threw my lunch away and went out to lunch with him. It was the start of a nearly five-year-long romance. When I left the factory to go back to college, he insisted on coming to Brooklyn to visit me at home on a Saturday. I knew what Mother's reaction would be, but he wouldn't take no for an answer.

The meeting was every bit as bad as I had feared. He came beautifully dressed, but in a sports coat and slacks. Even if Mother had not been primed to hate him on sight, that would have done it; to her, a gentleman wore a suit, and that was the end of the matter. She served tea and cakes with a maximum of ungraciousness and a minimum of conversation, and, after my suitor left, the battle began. It ended with my shouting, "Mother, I don't want to, but if you drive me to do it, I will pack up and leave!" We had an armed truce on the subject after that.

I remember her asking my father in that era, "Shirley's gettin' out of hand. Charles, what we gonna do?" My father, as always, tried to persuade Mother to be less of an islander and more American in her views. "She's only growing up," he assured her.

As a matter of fact I was grown up. I was going on twenty-one, and after a skinny adolescence I had blossomed into an attractive enough quiet little girl with long hair. My suitor and I began to date steadily; in a year or two we became engaged. Then the truth came out: my "fiancé" was married. He had a family in his native Jamaica he had never told me about. Almost as bad, I learned that he had been up to his eyebrows in an immigration fraud racket, helping bring people into the country with false birth certificates and then blackmailing them. Our "engagement" was broken, and shortly after that the Immigration and Naturalization Service arrested and deported him.

The shock lasted for months. I couldn't sleep; I couldn't eat. Far from plump to start with, I gradually became a skeleton. I considered suicide. I hated men and I always would. Life had nothing more to offer me that would ever be any good. Finally a doctor urged my family to get me out of town into the country. They took me to a farm in New Jersey, owned by old family friends.

In the quiet, surrounded by fresh air and affection, tempted by country cooking, I groped my way back to reality. When I came home I was physically normal again and in control of myself. I had decided that my future would be one of complete devotion to my profession of child welfare and early childhood education. And one of spinsterhood.

But although I did not know it, I had already met the really important man in my life, the one who was eventually going to persuade me, with infinite gentleness and patience, to change my mind about being a spinster. At Columbia one night, running from a class to a meeting as I was always doing, a stocky, quiet, handsome Jamaican named Conrad Chisholm had stopped me and persuaded me to stand still long enough to get acquainted.

When Conrad learned I was back in circulation, he began to lay siege. I used every tactic I knew to drive him away: glacial aloofness, standing him up, angry sarcasm, avoiding him. He refused to be shaken by anything I did. It took months, during which he often came to the house and, reversing the previous situation, my mother welcomed him and I ignored him. Eventually his calm determination and his inexhaustible sympathy got through to me. I realized that this was a different kind of man. We were married in 1949.

Probably few men could have stayed happily married to me for more than twenty years. I don't think Conrad has ever had a moment of insecurity or jealousy over the fact that I have always been a public figure. Thoughtless people have suggested that my husband would have to be a weak man who enjoys having me dominate him. They are wrong on both counts. Conrad is a strong, self-sufficient personality, and I do not dominate him. As a matter of fact, a weak man's feelings of insecurity would long since have wrecked a marriage like ours. Conrad is able to let me have the limelight without a thought; I thrive in it and he doesn't care for it. "Take the pictures of her," he tells photographers, and then ducks out of their range to stand at the side of the room, puffing his pipe.

Perhaps the only major decision of his life in which Conrad submitted to my insistence was when he left private investigative work to go to work in a related field for the city of New York. For most of his life, Conrad worked for a private security bureau, specializing in insurance claims cases. He is an accomplished actor and this, combined with his inexhaustible patience, made him an extremely effective agent in checking out claims of disability made by persons who may have exaggerated or misrepresented their injuries and incapacitation in the hope of bilking an insurance company. But the work was often dangerous, and I kept pressing him to change. Eventually he agreed, and became an investigator for the city, checking out the eligibility of Medicaid claimants.

A year after I gave up political involvement, my last and biggest job in education came to me. In 1959, I left the Hamilton-Madison Center to become a consultant to the City Division of Day Care. There I was responsible for general supervision of ten day care centers with ten directors, seventy-eight teachers, thirty-eight other employees, and a budget of $397,000. It was my job to study and evaluate the programs of day care agencies (not only the city ones), write reports on them, go to conferences, and run meetings to set standards for child care in New York City. Another major assignment was to promote the development of day care centers, a missionary job that meant endless meetings and talks to convince community leaders that the city's children needed more and better care facilities.

But in 1960 — I suppose it was inevitable — I was drawn back into politics. A group of about six persons, of whom I was one, formed a new organization that we named the Unity Democratic Club. Its goal was to do what the Bedford-Stuyvesant Political League had never managed to do: take over the entire Seventeenth Assembly District political organization and boot out the failing but still potent white machine.

That was a year of mounting rebellion all over the city. Reform Democratic clubs were trying to challenge regular clubs in many districts. In ours, there was a Nostrand Democratic Club of old-style insurgents — I mean that racial questions were not involved with their insurgency. Our fledgling organization made common cause with them, and the Unity Club's leader, Thomas R. Jones, a black attorney, ran for state assemblyman on the same ticket with the Nostrand Club's Joseph K. Rowe — a white man — for committeeman. They were opposing Samuel I. Berman, the machine's assemblyman, and Vincent Carney, the long-time Seventeenth District boss, for committeeman.

We made a lot of noise. We wrote Mayor Robert F. Wagner and demanded that he appoint more Negroes and Puerto Ricans to city jobs. Eleanor Roosevelt, then seventy-five years old, came to speak at a Jones-Rowe rally and drew 400 people, one of our biggest crowds. She was touring the city speaking for reform candidates. We got heavy labor support and had a star-studded list of sponsors on our letterhead that started with the name of Harry Belafonte. Our platform stressed integration, better schools, higher wages, more jobs, better health care, housing, and transportation, more lighting, sanitation, and youth services for the neighborhood, and full representation for black and Puerto Rican citizens.

They were all the causes that Mac Holder, some of the other leaders in the neighborhood, and I had been fighting for for years. Mac, by the way, was running against Assemblyman Bertram Baker, who was then Brooklyn's first and only black state legislator, in the Sixth Assembly District next door. Baker, a native of Nevis in the British West Indies, had managed a coup like the one we were attempting. He and his forces had thrown out the white bosses and he was sitting in the Assembly and in the councils of the Kings County Democratic organization, where his face and that of his co-leader were the only black ones.

The Unity and Nostrand clubs formed a Committee for Full Registration and Adequate Representation, and we started to recruit and train canvassers. We had instruction classes for them, stressing how to get signatures on petitions in legal form and how to get unregistered or lapsed voters to the polls to sign up. Some of them became volunteer poll watchers for us. The regular organization could hire all the help it wanted on Election Day at seven dollars for three hours' work. Our troops worked for nothing, and they made the regular election officials edgy and angry. Some of them threatened to call the police to get rid of our people looking over their shoulders. Our troops had been well briefed on the law and they weren't frightened. They told the organization flunkies to go right ahead and call the law.

To read Berman and Carney's election folders, you would have thought they were soul brothers. They were full of nothing but propaganda about how Berman had backed a resolution condemning the murder of Emmett Till, how Mississippi should be condemned for failing to punish the mob that killed Mack Parker, how Berman had supported the Metcalf-Baker Fair Housing Bill, how they were NAACP members, and so on and on and on.

Obviously they were pretty scared. But we didn't make it the first time. Berman beat Tom Jones 3082 votes to 2033, and Carney beat Rowe by a similar margin. Jones had drawn 42 percent of the vote.

We took a few deep breaths and started planning to do better in 1962. All through 1961 we were active. We held political education seminars, at which other speakers and I attacked the machine and kept selling the idea that we had a right to be represented by leaders of our own choice. We made analyses of the racial composition of each election district. We signed up more and more members in the Unity Club. By the spring of 1962 we had an organization that was at least the equal of the regular one.

This time we went for broke, on our own, running Tom Jones against Berman for both the Assembly seat and for district leader. Carney by this time had retired from politics and turned the committee seat over to Berman. The regulars ran a black woman, Carrie Lark, for district co-leader against our candidate, Ruth Goring.

We got the endorsement of the parent group of the city reform movement, the New York Committee for Democratic Voters. We thought we were going to have the backing of one of the three members of the "troika" that ran the county organization at that time, the Reverend Gardner C. Taylor, but Taylor switched away late in the primary compaign.

Our campaign literature this time let it all hang out. "End boss-ruled plantation politics!" one throwaway read. The white political writers cried "unfair" in their columns. "Close to libelous," one called our campaign. All the way through, they kept writing about our "racist tone." You could tell they were reflecting the panic of their perennial sources and best drinking buddies, the county bosses. We had more relevant things to talk about, such as a $1.50 minimum wage and more jobs for black and Puerto Rican workers at local stores, factories, and hospitals.

It had started out as a three-way primary, by the way. Mac Holder was also in it. The regulars concentrated their fire on us, hoping for Mac to split the black vote. They made a deal and put him on the ticket for committeeman, leaving Berman running only for the Assembly.

The Democratic bosses didn't like anything about our campaign. They even tried to make a fuss over the fact that the big sign over our headquarters on Bergen Street only listed Jones' name and those of the state candidates, without those of the three white congressmen and the white state senator whose districts also fell into ours.

None of it did them any good. On Primary Day in September, Jones beat Berman by 2714 to 2457 and beat Holder by 3042 to 2654. Mrs. Goring won as co-leader, and we were in, with 60 percent of the vote.

The white organization was dead at last in Bedford-Stuyvesant. Its leaders were out of office, and the Unity Democratic Club was the official Democratic organization for the district. The election was an anticlimax. The Republican and Liberal parties had nominees, but, as usual, they were no threat. Our slate won easily.

Tom Jones and Ruth Goring joined Bert Baker and his co-leader on the county committee, and there were now four blacks among its twenty-two members. It was far from enough, considering the huge black and Puerto Rican population in the borough, to be representative. But it was a historic step.

I was on the club's executive committee, just about back where I had started my political career. That seemed a little ironic, but of course there was an enormous difference. On the old 17th A.D. Club board, it had been just a game they were playing with me and I had known it and played it for what it was worth. This time I was one of the leaders of a group that was really representative of the district, and we were in a position, for the first time, to exert some leverage on the party and the state legislature in behalf of the people who had been second-class citizens all their lives.

Tom Jones served only one term in the Assembly. By 1964 a seat had opened up on the civil court bench in Brooklyn. The county organization, in a mood to make some accommodations with the black community, was willing to support him for it. Jones is an able and learned lawyer and was ideally suited for the bench. He deserved the opportunity. But before he agreed to accept the nomination, there were a few problems to clear up. One of them was Shirley Chisholm.

If Jones ran for judge, there was a vacancy in the state Assembly. I wanted it, and I told the club I felt I deserved it. This was unwelcome news to the county organization, and it did not appeal very much to some of the people in my own club. Some of the men fancied the nomination themselves. Others, who had had a taste of how I operated — a little woman who didn't know how to play the game or when to shut up — didn't want to see me in a position of any more importance than I already had.

For my part, I was not interested in listening to any reasons why I shouldn't run. By then I had spent about ten years in ward politics and had done everything else but run for office. Starting as a cigar box decorator, I had compiled voter lists, carried petitions, rung doorbells, manned the telephone, stuffed envelopes, and helped voters get to the polls. I had done it all to help other people get elected. The other people who got elected were men, of course, because that was the way it was in politics. This had to change someday, and I was resolved that it was going to start changing right then. I was the best-qualified nominee, and I was not going to be denied because of my sex.

With noticeable reluctance by some of the members, the Unity Democratic Club endorsed me. Jones went to the county organization to report, "Shirley Chisholm is our Assembly candidate." We were the regular organization, and what we decided should have been the end of it, according to the rule book.

But Tom Jones started to have misgivings. He was clearly under some pressure to reconsider giving up the Assembly seat, because that meant it would possibly come to me. But more than that, Jones was not basically a passive type, and he hated to give up active politics for the bench. He wavered briefly. But his family and friends urged him not to lose the opportunity of rising to the bench, and he finally went ahead.

I won the primary against token opposition, and my next problem was what to run my campaign with. The Unity Democratic Club had very little money although its organization would work for me, and that was invaluable. The county organization was not about to help us much. White clubs usually got more money than the black clubs. Mailings, posters, rallies, all the ways you get to the voters or get them out to hear you, cost money. I went to the bank four times that year and drew a total of $4000 from my savings. It's not much by modern standards, but I made it do.

I was not the first black woman ever to run for the Assembly in Brooklyn. In 1946 a Republican, Maude B. Richardson, ran and came within 200 votes of beating the Democrat, John Walsh. (In the wake of that scare, the machine had submitted to the nomination of Bertram Baker, the first black state legislator from Kings County.) But despite this precedent, I met with hostility because of my sex from the start of my first campaign. Even some women would greet me, "You ought to be home, not out here." Once, while I was collecting nominating petition signatures in the big Albany housing project — where Conrad and I had been captains for several years — one man about seventy lit into me. "Young woman, what are you doing out here in this cold? Did you get your husband's breakfast this morning? Did you straighten up your house? What are you doing running for office? That is something for men."

A direct counterattack would have achieved nothing. I handled all such hecklers, male and female, the same way. I told them calmly that I had been serving the community for a number of years and now I would appreciate an opportunity to serve it on a higher level, in elected office. Many persons, both men and women, I said, felt that I was the person to protect their interests and I would like a chance to run and try to win.

The old man signed my petition. So did some of the others. I never struck back at the black men who wanted to argue with me in that vein. I understood too well their reasons for lashing out at black women; in a society that denied them real manhood, I was threatening their shaky self-esteem still more.

As a matter of fact, there is as much — it could even be more — panic among white men confronted by an able, determined female who refuses to play the sex role they think is fitting. "Sexism" — to use Betty Friedan's coinage — has no color line. Sometimes they come straight out like the old man in the housing project and tell an upstart female that a woman's place is in the home. More often, their attack is indirect. They stress what are considered feminine foibles: "Women talk too much." "Women are illogical." "Women take everything personally." In politics, the men tell each other, "This isn't a game for women." Or, at parties, in asides that they allow one to hear, they talk about how "it has to be a certain kind of woman who goes in for politics . . ." By that they mean an easily manipulated type who will follow the dictates of the men. If possible, that is the kind they pick.

But getting back to the campaign, it was a long, hard summer and fall. I won by a satisfying margin, in a three-way contest, with 18,151 votes to 1893 for the Republican, Charles Lewis, and 913 for the Liberal, Simon Golar.

Nineteen sixty-four was the first big year for black candidates in New York State. Redistricting, forced by the Supreme Court's "one man, one vote" decision, had wiped out some of the cleverly drawn district lines that had split the black vote and kept white men in office. When I went to Albany I went as one of eight, six black assemblymen and two state senators, the largest number by far in history. I was the only woman, but not the first. Mrs. Bessie Buchanan had represented an Assembly district in Harlem for a time, about ten years earlier.

One thing marred the triumph. Papa had not lived to see it. He had died suddenly the year before. For years, he had suffered from mild hypertension. One morning after working out in the yard in the sun with no hat, he came in the house and told Mother, "Ruby, I have such a bad headache." Then he sat down in a chair and died of a general circulatory failure. I was at work at the City Division of Day Care. When I heard the news over the phone, I collapsed screaming and had to be given a sedative. My election would have made him so proud; it was even more than he had hoped for me.

Papa left a legacy of bad feeling in my family. Ever since I had been in grade school, we had always been the closest. We shared an interest in current events and politics that Mother and my sisters did not have. He and I talked more than he did with the other girls. It sometimes seemed that it was the two of us against my mother and my three sisters. Papa left no will, but before his death he had set up a trust fund for me, with what had been left of his savings after he bought the house. There was no way I could change the arrangement, and the jealousy it naturally caused has been a barrier between me and my family ever since.

6

In the State Assembly

I HAD BEEN up the Hudson to Albany about three times, leading delegations, before I made my first trip there as a state assemblywoman. My previous trips were poor preparation for what I found.

The same redistricting that had made it possible to elect the largest number of black legislators in the state's history had returned the Democrats to control of the Assembly, with their first majority in eight years. The New York Democratic party has an incredible knack for, as a witty political writer once put it, "snatching defeat from the jaws of victory." Its suicidal tendencies surfaced again in January 1965 as the Democratic majority in the Assembly began a historic and ridiculous two-month-long fight over who would be the Speaker. Both the contenders were from Brooklyn. Anthony Travia had been minority leader through the lean, Republican years and expected to remain the party's leader in the lower house. But Stanley Steingut, the Kings County Democratic chairman, also wanted the job, partly because his father Irwin had been Speaker in his day.

The system is the one common to most representative bodies in this country: the majority elects the body's presiding officer. But first the majority must unite behind one man. If it is split, and the opposition party votes for one of its own, which is normal, then no one has a majority.

The word was that Steingut had the votes. But by the second day of the session it became clear that there was going to be trouble. Stanley did not have the votes. Neither did Anthony Travia. County leaders came in from upstate and downstate to huddle with their people. There were endless caucuses at the Hotel DeWitt Clinton, where Democrats stayed during legislative sessions. Across the street at the Ten Eyck, the Republicans' hotel, there was great glee.

Most of the Democrats were from metropolitan New York and its suburbs. There was a party stronghold in Buffalo and another in Albany, but only a Democrat here and there in the rest of upstate. Every day the Brooklyn delegation caucused the Bronx delegation, the upstaters, and so on. Travia and Steingut each had a suite at the DeWitt. If a member on whose vote they were counting did not stop by their rooms every night sometime between 8:00 P.M. and midnight, they got worried and virtually sent out the dogs.

No one was paying any attention to me. I was a woman and a newcomer, and I was expected to accept the rules and follow tradition. The former assemblyman, Tom Jones, was close to Steingut, so everyone assumed that I would support him. No one invited me to any meetings or worried because I didn't check in nightly at the Steingut suite. They were confident that they had my vote. One day outside the Assembly chamber, a Brooklyn leader named Howard Shakin (a boy I went to school with — as a matter of fact, he used to copy from me) was giving me all the usual political talk, running down the votes Steingut had in his pocket, predicting that he would get it, and concluding, "It's a good thing to be on the winning side." I asked him, "Who told you I was going to vote for Stanley?"

"Everybody knows that," Howard said.

"Everybody but me."

"Aren't you?"

"I'm casting my vote for Anthony Travia."

"Oh, my God!" Howard said. "The delegation is counting on your vote. Practically the whole delegation is going with Stanley."

"All of you have a nerve assuming where my vote will go," I said. Then he gave me a warning I had heard before and have heard many times since. It always comes in portentous, funereal tones, often accompanied by a pointing finger.

"Shirley," Shakin said, "you'll be committing political suicide if you don't go along with us."

When the word got out, Travia asked to talk to me. "Are you really going to vote for me?" he asked. I told him it was true. "Why?" he said.

I told him I had been watching what went on in Albany. He had been minority leader for eight years, and from what reporters who covered him and legislators who worked with him said, he had earned an opportunity to head the party. Capitol employees told me how Travia came in early every morning and was regularly the last one out of the building at night. No one had given me any specific reason to vote against him. It was a pure power play. My stand was that unless he had not done the job of minority leader satisfactorily, or there was some derogatory evidence against him, we should not cast him aside.

The truth is I had never known Travia well, although we came from the same borough. Stanley and I had been feuding for years. Like most politicians, he could never accept my outspoken style. His opinion of me since then is probably expressed in stronger terms, but up to that point he would have said something like, "Shirley is a nice person. She's bright, but she doesn't play the rules of the game."

That is true. I don't, because I don't choose to. It is not because I don't know what the rules are. I have participated in and watched politics for more than twenty years, and I know how things are supposed to be done. I also know why the rules are made, and why they are enforced without mercy. Frederick Douglass said it best and shortest: "Power concedes nothing." The rules of the political game are designed to make it possible for men in power to control the actions of their supporters and stay there. If they can't control someone, they are disturbed. It is a threat to their security. They put the troublemaker's name in a figurative little black book, with a note: this is a person we have to hold back. They label him a rebel, a nonconformist, a maverick.

If I wasn't a maverick in the political power brokers' books before the Travia-Steingut face-off, I was from then on. As it turned out, my vote didn't matter one way or the other in breaking the deadlock. I hadn't expected it to. I voted the way I did for a reason that would not occur to a good many legislators — because I knew it was right. It would have been wrong to turn out Anthony Travia, just wrong. He had led the party's battles when it was a minority, putting in uncounted hours to organize and prepare for debate against the Republicans. To the extent that anyone outside Brooklyn took note of my "defection," they probably put it down to some kind of a deal. Travia had gotten to me and promised me something more than Steingut, people may have thought. There was no deal. The truth was much simpler.

For two months the legislature was crippled by the deadlock. The state senate, Republican controlled, could do nothing with the lower house immobilized, and the Assembly could do nothing until it had elected officers. The Republicans' delight turned into irritation, and finally they did an unprecedented thing. They settled the issue by casting their votes for Travia. Steingut had every vote in the Brooklyn delegation except mine and Bertram Baker's. Baker had made a stirring seconding speech for Travia, and I made one too, although as a freshman I should have kept quiet.

Travia and I got along well after that, but not as well as one might expect. Like everyone else, he couldn't control my actions, and sometimes this bothered him. The Democratic power structure began to understand that I was not going to be reliable. Its leaders were asking, "What does she want?" It was a little like the old Seventeenth Assembly District Democratic Club all over again. Here I was, on the inside; I had made it, I was one of the select group. Why didn't I act the way everyone else did?

I told Travia at the start, "Although I support you, there will be times I will disagree with you." Politicians always think if you align yourself with them on one issue, you're with them from then on. They never could predict what I would do.

Most black politicians are no different from white ones. They're not their own bosses either. If they don't function within the framework, they're punished and, if possible, eliminated. The punishment is drastic. They assign you to committees that are not popular, or where no work is done. They don't invite you in on things, from dinner parties to drafting bills. Your own bills are doomed; bosses can tell a chairman to keep them bottled up in committee, or, if they get out, it only takes a hint dropped on the floor that the leadership would like to see this bill not pass.

The strange thing is that this hasn't happened to me, and I sometimes wonder why. Maybe I am just lucky, but being a maverick hasn't kept me from being an effective legislator. One reason may be that there is a lot more to a party than its leadership. Many of my colleagues who do not agree at all with some of my thinking will, on specific issues, sometimes "give me a vote." That's the phrase they use: "Can you give me a vote on this?" I think they feel that there is no personal vindictiveness in my rebellions, that I am only fighting hard for things I believe in strongly, so they respect me as a person even when I horrify them as a politician. "You know, Chisholm," one man in Albany said to me, "I think you're wrong; but you're sincere, I've got to give you that."

Out of fifty bills I introduced in the legislature, eight passed, a high score if one knows how many bills are introduced in Albany at every session and how few even reach the floor.

Two I was especially satisfied with. One created a program called SEEK, to make it possible for young men and women from disadvantaged backgrounds to go to college, by seeking them out and assisting them while they go to school. A nationwide program on the same design is urgently needed, instead of the fantastic, long-term debt arrangement with which the Nixon administration thinks it could meet some of the same needs. The other was a bill to set up the state's first unemployment insurance coverage for personal and domestic employees. Every employer who paid $500 or more had to make contributions to the unemployment insurance fund. It passed in my first year, and so did two of my other bills. One corrected an outrageous legal discrimination against women schoolteachers. If pregnancy interrupted their careers, they lost their tenure rights. My bill changed that.

The other black member with whom I worked most closely was Assemblyman Percy Sutton, now the Manhattan borough president, a man I came to admire greatly. The Associated Press called us the two most militant and effective black members of the Assembly.

In four years I had to run for reelection twice, in 1965 and 1966. They kept changing the district lines. I have always wondered if they weren't doing it just to keep me off balance and on the run. Each time I had a primary fight, so that really made six campaigns in four years, counting the first ones. In both 1965 and 1966, after I won the primaries, I went into the general election with Liberal endorsement. In 1965, I beat the Republican, Fred F. Shaw, Jr., with 10,508 to 2277. In 1966 my opponent was Jesse L. Vann, and I won by 9743 to 2372.

The 1965 New York legislative session was one of the most productive in years, but not everything it did was good. It passed a law that violated the state and federal constitutions — and I say that despite the fact that courts have tortured their reasoning into saying that it did not — a bill to give state money to help church-run schools. I made a strong speech against the law, and voted with the minority when the bill rolled through the Assembly 136 to 18. "We are gradually eroding the public school system," I warned. "Each of us is going to have to make a very crucial decision soon as to whether or not we believe in the separation of church and state — whether we believe in our Constitution."

A bill of mine to provide state aid to day care centers had passed earlier, and also another to raise from $500 to $600 the maximum amount of spending per pupil by a local school toward which the state would pay a share. In addition to the constitutional question, there was a practical reason for opposing aid to church schools. The amount of money available for state aid is not unlimited, and it should be reserved for the schools that educate the children of any and all of the people. If a minority group wants to maintain its own schools for its own purposes, there should be no interference with them, provided the schools meet academic standards. But

they have no right to public money, which should go to the
public schools. They should support their private schools
with private money.

One bill that I introduced should become law in every
state, but unfortunately it did not succeed even in New York.
It would have made it mandatory for policemen to successfully complete courses in civil rights, civil liberties, minority
problems, and race relations before they are appointed to a
police department.

During four years in Albany, I had a liberal education in
how politics is run in our country — a sort of graduate course
to follow my basic education in ward and county politicking.
I did not like a great deal of what I learned.

New York State legislators are part-time lawmakers. Most
of them, of course, are lawyers, but whatever they do for a
living, all those not retired have a job back home that is
likely to be their main concern. For many, the legislative session is as much like a convention as it is a serious business.
There is an active, shall we say, night life. I took no part in
it, in spite of the fact that a few of the male legislators made
persistent and sometimes ingenious efforts to get me to. I
stayed in my room at the DeWitt Clinton, studying legislation and preparing for debates, and on weekends — which
usually started on Thursday nights — I went home to Brooklyn.

In Albany I first saw something I have since seen in Washington: men whose consciences urged them to one course of
action were forced to take another by the political dynamics
of a situation. A man might be against a bill, but one phone
call from a boss, advising him that his political future rests
on his being for the bill, would turn him around. I have even
seen a man cry because he was not permitted to do what he
knew was right.

It is what the system does. There are so many ways for those in power to control someone who strays. They jealously guard their power and use it to make sure that they call the shots; they are the ones who benefit from the system.

Another lesson I learned was that if you decide to operate on the basis of your conscience, rather than your political advantage, you must be ready for the consequences and not complain when you suffer them. There is little place in the political scheme of things for an independent, creative personality, for a fighter. Anyone who takes that role must pay a price.

In spite of this, I did manage to get some important things done in Albany. Was I less effective than I would have been if I had worked scrupulously within the system and played by all the rules? I don't think so. People who do that may be tossed a few bones, but their compromising really gets them nowhere. They make all the concessions, the bosses make none.

In Albany I learned how the processes of representative government work — or do not work. Often it was their failure that I saw. I do not want anyone to conclude that I have given up hope for our representative democracy; I have not, or I would not be where I am. It is because I value the idea so much that I am often keenly disappointed by the reality. So many times I saw that a majority understood there was a need to get something done, but nothing got done because of cumbersome, obsolescent legislative apparatus geared to the nineteenth century. I was not the only one in Albany frustrated at not being able to accomplish more.

But all this prepared me consummately well for Washington. That lesson was what I needed before I became a congresswoman.

7

Running for Congress

I T WAS ANOTHER REDISTRICTING that made it possible for me to run for Congress. Brooklyn had been gerrymandered outrageously. The black vote had been split four ways into districts where black voters were snowed under and had nothing to say about the election of Representatives Edna Kelly, Emanuel Celler John Rooney, and Frank Brasco. Mrs. Kelly's district was horseshoe shaped, almost as weird a creation as the Massachusetts district drawn by Elbridge Gerry in the nineteenth century. A Boston political cartoonist added claws and eyes to that one and christened it a new mythological beast, the "Gerrymander." If the word had not existed, it would have been necessary to invent it to describe the congressional map designed to disenfranchise minorities, especially blacks, in New York City before the middle nineteen sixties. After the Supreme Court ruled that districts must be of equal size and "compact and contiguous," that kind of outrageous districting disappeared (although the map makers are getting used to the new rules and are managing to invent new outrages without breaking them).

About 85 percent of Edna Kelly's district went into the

new Twelfth New York Congressional District. She decided to stay with the smaller part and run against Manny Celler. She lost. Meanwhile, nine or ten people were eyeing the Democratic nomination to the new Twelfth District seat in the House. City Councilman William C. Thompson, a former state senator, and the Reverend Milton Galamison, the NAACP leader, were among them. So was I.

The Kings County machine said it was going to keep its hands off the new "black" district and leave the choice of a nominee "up to the people." It sounded fine, but since when did a machine leave the choice of an important office up to the people? Shortly before Christmas 1967, months before the primary, a citizens' committee formed itself in the district. Their main concern was to prevent the choice of the kind of "Tom" that would appeal to the county organization.

The citizens' committee invited many of the potential candidates to come in for interviews, including me. I was the only woman. After all the interviews were over, they unanimously endorsed me. It was a big surprise. I had, I knew, been the only one of the potential candidates who talked back and disagreed with them about things they had said they would have to expect from a nominee. That was the reason they decided to pick me. Above everything, they wanted someone who would have the independence to refuse to be run by the machine. I did not go to them with my hat in my hand, and that was what they liked.

After the word leaked out, the politicians groaned. "If we couldn't control her in Albany, how are we going to in Washington?" The county organization, of course, did not abide by its pious intention to "leave it in the hands of the people." This was from the start their cop-out on endorsing me. It soon became well known in political circles and then in the district generally that Thompson was the organization's choice. The county machine never did endorse a candidate, but every action of its people showed, to the most unsophisticated resident of Bedford-Stuyvesant, that William C. Thompson was their man. White people think black people are stupid, but it came through to the community that the organization could not bring itself to endorse me because I would not submit to being bossed by any of them. It was interesting that, even among themselves, they never questioned my competence or dedication. What they said was always that I was "hard to handle."

Bertram Baker, my fellow assemblyman, wanted to get Thompson, who had taken his seat as district committeeman. But Baker was not going to back me because in our Assembly days we had crossed swords over a bill regulating pawnbrokers. I had implied that he was in league with the pawnbrokers, who prey on residents of the ghettos, against a bill that could crack down on the loan sharks. There must have been enough truth in it to hurt, because Baker was my enemy for a while. He backed a woman labor organizer, Mrs. Dolly Robinson, who had run for office several times but never won.

The eight leaders of the four Assembly districts in the new congressional district sat down with the county leaders to pick a candidate. "Shirley has never been disciplined," most of them agreed. The people, whom they had said they were going to let decide, had endorsed me, but that didn't matter. I had worked for the community for twenty years, but that didn't matter. They were unable to control me in any way. The white power structure would lose more of its grip on the black political organizations with me in Washington. That was what really mattered.

Tom Fortune's vote and my own (I had succeeded Ruth Goring as co-leader) were the only ones I got. The organization was against me. Its choice, William C. Thompson, at first assured me he was not going to run and would back me. But he changed his mind and announced one day before the circulation of petitions.

With Thompson and Dolly Robinson in, I faced a three-way primary. The Unity Democratic Club was for me; it was the base from which I started. Then a surprising thing happened: I had a call from Mac Holder.

My old-time mentor and enemy in recent years wanted to work for me. Twenty years back, he had said he wanted to live to elect a black judge and a black congressman. Now he thought he saw a chance of reaching the second, greater goal with me but, he told me, I couldn't win without him and the people in the streets. Looking back on it, I think he was right.

Mac told me, "You're the easiest product to sell and I'm going to organize the campaign and sell you." He worked nineteen hours a day to do it.

The days I put in were just as long. I almost killed myself because I wanted to show the machine that a little black woman was going to beat it. Quite possibly no one but Mac and I — and Conrad and the people — believed I could do it. The organization believed, from its past experience and because the political columnists told it so, that it would win because it was the organization and it had what it took to deliver the votes in a primary. I don't know whether Bertram Baker and Dolly Robinson really believed Dolly could win; perhaps they did, but it seemed to me that the real reason Bert had put up his own candidates was that he was not working for the organization. The party bosses were pleased with his candidate; they figured she would cut into my vote and assure Thompson's nomination.

So starting in February, I spent ten months doing the only thing I could do: I tramped the streets of Williamsburg, Crown Heights, and Bedford-Stuyvesant, telling my story to the people. I didn't have the money for a conventional congressional campaign; I had to make up for it with hard work. But I was determined to show them. People had to know that it was possible for someone with decency and a fighting spirit to overcome the system by beating it with its own weapons. For years in Brooklyn and New York City and Albany, I had watched the rotten political system that stands in the way of change, because its operators are beneficiaries of the status quo. They are committed against change, because they have things wired for their benefit now; changing the system to benefit the people more would mean that they would not be the kingmakers and wheeler-dealers any longer, these men who put themselves forward as leaders and guardians of the people. This is the insidious thing we have to fight.

So I campaigned the hard way, in the streets. Indoors, with a selected audience, you have control. But out on the street corners with the people, in the housing projects, in parks, you are under fire constantly. If you are insincere or have something to hide, you will be found out.

I wrote a slogan that said it all: "Fighting Shirley Chisholm — Unbought and Unbossed." I hammered on this. The weekends were the precious time. On Friday nights and through Sunday evenings, led by Thomas R. Fortune, my district leader, I traveled with a caravan of twenty to fifty cars manned by volunteers — men, women, and children. On both sides of each car we put a picture with the legend VOTE FOR CHISHOLM FOR CONGRESS — UNBOUGHT AND UNBOSSED. We had shopping bags with the same inscriptions. All week long, on the street, in markets, at clinics, you could see people with my shopping bags. We gave them out to everyone who would take them, with a package of material on my biography and Assembly record and a souvenir — a pen or a handkerchief — inside. The main stops were at housing projects; there are ten big ones in the district. We also stopped at churches, at parks, and on street corners to talk to anyone who would listen. I shook hands, answered questions, and listened to what the people had to say.

During the week I went to endless little house parties and teas given by women. In the black neighborhood I ate chitlins, in the Jewish neighborhood bagels and lox, in the Puerto Rican neighborhood arroz con pollo. We contacted every neighborhood woman leader we could find. "Bring your women in," I would urge them. Sometimes a woman would tell me that she would like to have a party for me, but she just couldn't afford it, and I would provide the money. I went to all kinds of homes. I wasn't interested in style.

While I was campaigning in the streets and living rooms of the district, Willie Thompson was so sure he would win with the organization behind him that he was up at Cape Cod vacationing. White leaders who had said they were going to keep their hands off were going around working for him. He felt secure because of the proportionate higher white vote as contrasted to the black vote, although numerically the district had a greater number of black and Puerto Rican voters.

When they counted the primary votes, with a very small turnout, I won by about 1000 votes. Dolly Robinson, as it resulted, didn't cut into my vote; if anything, into Willie's. I carried the four white districts.

Immediately after the primary, I became seriously ill, completely without warning. By this time my Republican opponent was in the field: James Farmer, the former national chairman of CORE, the Congress of Racial Equality. The New York Republicans had seen a golden opportunity in the new black Brooklyn district, and figured he was just the man to cash in on it for them. Of course, he didn't live in Brooklyn and never had, but there is no law that said he had to; he only had to live in New York State. He rented an apartment in the district for appearances' sake and tucked the nomination in his pocket.

Farmer's campaign was well oiled; it had money dripping all over it. He toured the district with sound trucks manned by young dudes with Afros, beating tom-toms: the big, black, male image. He drew the television cameramen like flies, a big national figure, winding up to become New York City's second black congressman (after Adam Clayton Powell). His people were flooding the streets. The television stations ignored the little female who was running against him. One station I called to complain to came right out and told me why. "Who are you?" the man asked. "A little schoolteacher who happened to go to the Assembly."

The trouble was, I had been sleeping very little because I had to get up so many times each night. Finally, Conrad bullied me into going to a doctor. I had to miss three important meetings, and I was fussing and carrying on all the way there.

"Either you're pregnant or you have a tumor," the doctor said as soon as he looked at me.

"Doc, you'd better know what you're talking about," I told him, "because I am running for Congress and I am not going to have a baby."

He examined me thoroughly and dropped all pretense at humor. "You've got to take her to a gynecologist and a surgeon tonight," he told Conrad, and he picked up the telephone. "I'm sending over Congresswoman Chisholm," he told the specialist at the other end of the line, "the young black woman who is going to be the congressman. I'm quite sure she has a massive tumor." It was the first time I was ever called "congressman," and I still wonder why he said it.

I couldn't believe it. He wasn't even asking me. I couldn't go. I had meetings that night. I had had no pain (although it had been growing for two years). As it turned out, it was concealed in the pelvic basin, the one spot where it would not have hurt much.

All night, waiting for the results of the tests, I couldn't sleep. I knew I had cancer. It was malignant, of course it was, I kept thinking.

If it had been, I would probably be dead now. The biopsy showed no malignancy. But all the same, they had to operate. That meant I had to interrupt all my appointments and put the campaign on ice. It was impossible, and I was mad. "Look, Doc," I said, "I've had it for two years. Can't I carry it a little longer, until after November?" But the doctor and Conrad were very firm. I went to Maimonides Hospital in late July.

The anesthetic was having no effect as they wheeled me into the operating room. I was so determined not to have the operation that I refused to go to sleep. But when I realized I was still wide awake and the operation was imminent, I screamed out. The doctor was startled. "Shirley?" he said. Then he ordered, "Two in her spine and one in her arm." That did it. I woke up with an incredibly long transverse incision, sewn up with what are called "Hollywood stitches." "No one will know it, even when you wear a bikini," the doctor assured me. They had given me such a large dose of anesthetic that I didn't come to for thirteen hours. Conrad was walking up and down and sweating all that time. He knew I must be dead. The next day I was walking around the hospital. I was determined to get back on the streets.

It was August, though, when I got home. I looked at myself in the mirror and wept. I was so emaciated from the waist down that I looked like Twiggy.

Farmer had been busy all this time. He was starting to ask, "Where's Mrs. Chisholm? We haven't seen or heard from her." The weather was hot, a city August, unbearable outdoors. I called the doctor and said, "Look, the stitches aren't in my mouth. I'm going out."

He argued until he realized it wasn't going to do any good. "If anything happens to you, don't call me," he said.

I took a big beach towel and wrapped it around my hips so my clothes wouldn't fall off. With that, I looked pretty good. Conrad had two women caring for me. I bribed them and called three men to come and take me out on the sound truck. We lived on the third floor then, and I had to walk down three flights. I told the biggest one, "You walk in front so if I fall I'll fall on you, and the other two can hold me." We went out. "Ladies and gentlemen," I said on the loudspeakers, "this is Fighting Shirley Chisholm and I'm up and around in spite of what people are saying."

The amazing thing is that from that day on I never had any repercussions from the operation. My doctor looks at me sometimes and says, "Any other woman would have collapsed." But it was what I had to do, so I did it.

There is one incident of the campaign I will never forget. Soon after the primary, before the operation, a woman rang my doorbell, and when I answered it she pushed an envelope into my hand. "This is the first, Chisholm," she said. There was $9.69 in the envelope, and I learned that she had collected it from a group of people on welfare at a bingo party. I sat down and cried. After she left, I told Conrad, "If I ever had any doubts, I don't now." My campaign was financed that way, and out of my own pocket. I set up my own headquarters, at 1103 Bergen Street. Before that time, at Unity Democratic Club headquarters, girls had been typing labels for mailings to registered voters. Then Tom Fortune would put them in an envelope and send them to me, with the number of each district on the outside. One day Mac looked at four of the district envelopes and figured we were at least 9000 names short. I checked one election district where there should have been 470 labels. There were only about ninety. What had happened, as it turned out, was that the girls who were doing the typing had skipped all the hard names — the long Italian ones they had trouble spelling, and so on. But in the heat of the campaign, when every snag becomes a crisis, this failure by our own supporters, who should have checked carefully the number of labels commensurate with the number of voters on the registration books, became a major thing. Mac told me, with his voice breaking, "Shirley, they don't want you either. But as long as I'm alive, you will go to Congress. This is what they want, the white bosses and the would-be black bosses, but you're not going to fall into their trap." So Mac took an unpaid leave from his job as statistician for the Brooklyn district attorney's office, and we got our own people, typewriters, and mimeograph machines and set up a campaign headquarters. He organized a regular assembly line for mailings. At details, there is no one like Mac. He seemed to remember everything. "That is how you keep your mind free for the important matters," he told me.

But Mac's important contribution to the campaign was not in organization alone. It came when I found that Farmer and his people were using my sex against me. To the black men — even some of those supposedly supporting me — sensitive about female domination, they were running me down as a bossy female, a would-be matriarch. I was not running an antimale campaign. The issue had never been a major one in my Assembly campaigns; there had been problems of my sex, but it was never a major theme of my opposition; nor had I ever thought to use it as an asset. But that was exactly what wise and wily Mac realized I had going for me. He had studied the voter rolls and found that for each man registered in the district there were 2.5 women. This is something not found in white communities. He and I realized that what Farmer thought was his strength was his Achilles' heel.

Men always underestimate women. They underestimated me, and they underestimated the women like me. If they had thought about it, they would have realized that many of the homes in black neighborhoods are headed by women. They stay put, raise their families — and register to vote in greater numbers. The women are always organizing for something, even if it is only a bridge club. They run the PTA, they are the backbone of the social groups and civic clubs, more than the men. So the organization was already there. All I had to do was get its help. I went to the presidents and leaders and asked, "Can you help me?" If I succeeded in convincing them, they were ready to help — and able.

It was not my original strategy to organize womanpower to elect me; it was forced on me by the time, place, and circumstances. I never meant and never mean to start a war between women and men. It is true that women are second-class citizens, just as black people are. Tremendous amounts of talent are being lost to our society just because that talent wears a skirt. This is stupid and wrong, and I want the time to come when we can be as blind to sex as we are to color. But that time is not here, and when someone tries to use my sex against me, I delight in being able to turn the tables on him, as I did in my congressional campaign.

Discrimination against women in politics is particularly unjust, because no political organization I have seen could function without women. They do the work that the men won't do. I know, because I have done it all. For years I stayed in the wings and worked to put men in office, even writing their speeches and cuing them on how to answer questions. They would still be exploiting my abilities if I had not rebelled. Increasingly, other women are reaching the same conclusion.

Less important than the sex issue was another undercurrent that ran against me. An inescapable fact, but one I have never liked to discuss because of the senseless bad feeling it can cause, is that a surprising number of the successful black politicians of our time are of West Indian descent. Thomas Jones, Ruth Goring, William Thompson, and I were all of Barbadian descent. State Senator Walter Stewart of Brooklyn is a Panamanian. So are many prominent blacks elsewhere in politics and the arts. In Brooklyn I have heard people grumbling for years, "They're taking over everything." Other black people will say, "Why don't those monkeys get back on a banana boat?" There is a strong undercurrent of resentment, at least in New York, where most of the islanders migrated. It has never come out in the open against me, but sometimes I can sense it.

It is wrong, because the accident that my ancestors were brought as slaves to the islands while black mainland natives' ancestors were brought as slaves to the States is really not important, compared to the common heritage of black brotherhood and unity in the face of oppression that we have. But the feeling is there. One basis for it may be that in the islands, slavery was a less destructive experience than it was in the States. Families were not broken up as they were in the South. The abolition of slavery came earlier there, and with much less trouble. In the islands, there have never been the same kind of race barriers. There are class barriers, but they are not the same; race lines cut across them. As a result, I think blacks from the islands tend to have less fear of white people, and therefore less hatred of them. They can meet whites as equals; this is harder for American blacks, who tend to overreact by jumping from feeling that whites are superior to looking down on them as inferior. Both attitudes equally isolate them from the greater society in which eventually we all have to learn to live.

Besides my women's organizations, I had other assets that Mr. Farmer and his big Republican backers had not counted on. One was my fluency in Spanish, my minor in college. At first, I was more confident of support in the Puerto Rican communities than the black ones. The results bore me out. I carried the Spanish-speaking sections of the district decisively.

Farmer and I had several public debates. I'm sure that he expected the contrast between his muscular, male assurance and poise and his opponent's little schoolteacher appearance would do him a lot of good. It turned out the other way. When I get on a platform, I am transformed; I have even been called Messianic! At any rate, people know I'm there. In our first debate at Pratt Institute, Farmer came out with enormous self-confidence. Before the evening was over, I could see he was getting worried.

Since then I have heard that he still thinks he outshone me in the debates. Somebody must not have thought so, because I beat him in the November election 2½ to 1. He had the Liberal endorsement, but even so I drew 34,885 votes to his 13,777 combined. A Conservative party candidate named Ralph J. Carrane got 3771.

8

Breaking the Rules

WHEN THE 91ST SESSION of the United States Congress convened, I arrived a little late and broke one of the venerable traditions of the House before I was even sworn in as a member. They had just finished calling the roll when I got there, so I rushed onto the floor with my coat and hat on. At least three members told me that I was breaking a House rule. I went back to a cloakroom to leave my hat and coat and returned to take the oath.

There was nothing like the decorum I had experienced the first day in the New York State Assembly. Members walked around shaking hands and slapping each other on the back, talking without paying any attention to the proceedings. Up behind a raised platform high in the front of the room sat a gaunt, frail-looking old man, Speaker John McCormack. I was shocked by the way the members milled around and set up a din that drowned out both the Speaker and the men who were taking turns giving brief speeches. The speechmakers were talking on an incredible variety of subjects that seemed of no importance to me. Each talked for one minute, then broke off and handed a copy of his speech to a clerk. The next day it would be printed in full in the *Congressional Record* as if it had been really given and the other members had listened to it.

Only a few of the faces were known to me, but everyone knew who I was. They were cordial, but in many greetings I sensed aloofness. Men kept asking me, "What does your husband think about all this?" They acted as if they were joking, but they meant to imply that, after all, "a woman's place . . ." I told them all that this was nothing new for Conrad and me; we had met while I was running from one meeting to another; during the early years of our marriage when he worked as a private detective, he was often away from home; then when he became an investigator for the city and was home every night I was away in the state Assembly four days a week, so my being in Washington four days a week would be nothing new.

After several weeks I realized that everyone had been expecting someone else, a noisy, hostile, antiwhite type. Some of my new colleagues admitted it frankly. "You're not the way we thought you'd be," one said. "You're actually charming."

When the campaign ended, I had taken three weeks' vacation in Jamaica, sleeping and eating, trying to gain back a few pounds. Ten months of campaigning, broken up by a major operation, had drained my vitality. I knew I should be in Washington rounding up a staff, but first I had to have some rest. When I came to Washington in December, I had to do everything at once. I interviewed a string of applicants for my office staff. Many new congressmen reward their supporters by putting them in staff jobs. I knew from my experience in Albany that this would be a mistake. What I needed was experience, to make up for my own inexperience in Washington, and after that, of course, I needed competence and loyalty. Before long, I decided my staff would be composed of young women, for the most part, from the receptionist to my top assistants. Capitol Hill offices swarm with intelligent, Washington-wise, college-trained — and attractive — young women who do most of the work that makes a congressman look good, but often get substandard pay for it and have little hope of advancing to a top staff job. The procedure in my office, I decided, would be different. I have never regretted it. Since then, I have also hired some outstanding young men, on my district and Washington staffs, but the majority is still female. More than half are black, but there has been pressure on me from some of my constituents to hire an all-black staff. "If you don't, who will?" I have been asked. What I have done is to hire the best applicants I can get. If they are black, so much the better. But the young white women on my staff are every bit as dedicated and hard working. Even the most suspicious folks from Bedford-Stuyvesant, once they come in contact with them and see how they are working for me and my district, are won over. One constituent paid one of the girls what he thought was the ultimate compliment. "She's black inside," he said.

The first big event in a freshman congressman's career is his assignment to a committee. He is not likely to get the one he wants because length of service, seniority, counts more than anything else and there are several hundred more senior members ahead of him. But for the sake of courtesy the leaders of his party ask him which one he prefers. Democrats in the House leave the power to assign members to committees in the hands of the fifteen Democrats who form the majority of the Ways and Means Committee. The Republicans have a special Committee on Committees that does the same thing. Why they need so many people to do the job is hard to understand. The only criterion that matters in picking members for committee vacancies is their length of service in Congress. Congress calls it the seniority system.

I call it the senility system.

My first choice, naturally, was the Education and Labor Committee, because I am an educator and because I had worked on and for educational legislation in the New York State Assembly. There were some vacancies on the Democratic side, and it would have made sense to take advantage of my twenty years' experience in education by appointing me to one of them. Next I would have liked to have been appointed to the Banking and Currency Committee, because it holds the purse strings for housing construction, and, next to education and employment, housing is the major need of poor people, black and white. The Post Office and Civil Service Committee would also have been relevant to my interests to some extent. A large part of post office employees are blacks or from other minority groups. Failing all those, I would have welcomed appointment to the Government Operations Committee. I thought it would be a chance to satisfy my curiosity about how government decisions are made and how federal money is spent.

New York's representative on the Democratic committee is Representative Jacob H. Gilbert of the Bronx. He assured me that he would try to get me an education committee seat. I sent a letter with a resumé of my background to every majority member of Ways and Means.

The committee meetings are held behind guarded doors, but it is impossible to keep that many congressmen from talking afterward. I learned by the grapevine that the committee had met and assigned me to the Agriculture Committee. Gilbert assured me he had tried to get me a better assignment, but other members confided that he hadn't tried very hard.

The Agriculture Committee sounded like a ridiculous

assignment for a black member from one of the country's most deprived city neighborhoods, but as a matter of fact it might not have been completely out of line. I had grown up on a farm (although I'm sure no one on the Committee on Committees knew that when they gave me the assignment; I probably just got what was left over after the other assignments had been made). But more than that, the committee has jurisdiction over food stamp and surplus food programs and is concerned with migrant labor — subjects with which I am concerned and to which I could make a contribution.

Then I found out what my subcommittee assignments were to be: rural development and forestry. Forestry! That did it. I called Speaker McCormack. The only time I had ever talked to the Speaker was a few days earlier. He had come over to the Capitol Hill Hotel, where I was holding a reception for a large group of people from Brooklyn, to administer the oath of office to me before the group. He had sworn me in earlier that day, with the other first-year members, as the House began its first session of the new Congress, but he had gracefully agreed to come to the hotel and repeat the ceremony for my neighbors and friends, for whom there had not been room enough in the spectators' gallery.

"I don't know if this is protocol, Mr. Speaker," I told him, "but I wanted to talk to you because I feel my committee and subcommittee assignments do not make much sense." John McCormack was cordial and sympathetic. His manners never fail him. Could he help me get my assignment changed to one with some relevance to my district?

"Mrs. Chisholm, this is the way it is," the Speaker said. "You have to be a good soldier."

After I was a good soldier for a few years, my reward would come, he assured me.

"All my forty-three years I have been a good soldier," I said.

"The time is growing late, and I can't be a good soldier any longer. It does not make sense to put a black woman representative on a subcommittee dealing with forestry. If you do not assist me, I will have to do my own thing."

The Speaker was startled for the first time. "Your what?"

"It means I will do what I have to do, regardless of the consequences. Doing your thing means that if you have strong feelings about something, you do it."

What he thought I meant, I will never know. Probably he was afraid I would start some disturbances. He said he would talk to Wilbur Mills, the chairman of the Ways and Means Committee.

Mr. Mills, the Arkansas Democrat who is absolute ruler of one of the most powerful committees on the Hill, did not like it that a freshman had complained about his assignment, and had even gone over his head to do it. What the two of them said, I never found out, but they agreed to ask Agriculture Committee Chairman W. R. Poage of Texas whether I could have a different subcommittee. Mills had been annoyed, but Poage, I heard later, really blew his stack and made some very unpleasant remarks.

There was one avenue of attack left. The committee assignments still had to be approved by the full Democratic majority at a caucus. I appealed to some of the more experienced members for advice on how to move that my assignment be reconsidered. Representative Brock Adams of Washington coached me but warned, "The way they operate, you won't get recognized to make your motion."

He was almost right. Every time I rose, two or three men jumped up. The senior member standing is always recognized first, so they never got to me. They probably expected that I would be discouraged after a while. Men were smiling and nudging each other as I stood there trying to get the floor.

After six or seven attempts, I walked down an aisle to the "well," the open space between the front row of seats and the Speaker's dais, and stood there. I was half afraid and half enjoying the situation, as Mr. Mills, who was in the chair, conferred with the majority leader, Carl Albert of Oklahoma. They must have been talking about what to do with me, because after the huddle ended I was recognized.

"For what purpose is the gentlewoman from New York standing in the well?" Mr. Mills asked.

"I'd been trying to get recognized for half an hour, Mr. Chairman," I said, "but evidently you were unable to see me, so I came down to the well. I would just like to tell the caucus why I vehemently reject my committee assignment."

I had a short speech prepared. It said that even though I had spent twenty years in education and served on the Education Committee of the New York Assembly for four years, I understood that geography and seniority make it difficult for a first-term representative to get his first choice of a committee assignment.

"But I think it would be hard to imagine an assignment that is less relevant to my background or to the needs of the predominantly black and Puerto Rican people who elected me, many of whom are unemployed, hungry, and badly housed, than the one I was given."

I pointed out that there were only nine black members of the House, although in terms of the percentage of the population that is black there should be more than forty (I underestimated — I should have said fifty-five). So, I said, the House leadership "has a moral duty to somewhat right the balance by the putting of the nine members it has in positions where they can work effectively to help this nation meet its critical problems of racism, deprivation, and urban decay." Then I offered a resolution removing me from the Agriculture Committee and directing the Committee on Committees to come back to the next monthly caucus with a different assignment for me.

My amendment created a parliamentary problem of some kind, and Mr. Mills asked me to withdraw it on the assurance that he would recognize me to offer it later. I did, and he was as good as his word. It passed.

Several of the male members spoke to me afterward in sympathetic terms, as if I had just had a death in the family. "You've committed political suicide," one advised me. That phrase sort of made me feel at home.

"The leadership will have it in for you as long as you're here," I was warned. What puzzled me and made me angry was that some of these men really agreed with me. "You're right, we need change around here," they said. But what they didn't say, and perhaps did not realize they were revealing, was that they didn't dare to fight for it themselves.

It is incomprehensible to me, the fear that can affect men in political offices. It is shocking the way they submit to forces they know are wrong and fail to stand up for what they believe. Can their jobs be so important to them, their prestige, their power, their privileges so important that they will cooperate in the degradation of our society just to hang on to those jobs?

The seniority system keeps a handful of old men, many of them southern whites hostile to every progressive trend, in control of the Congress. These old men stand implacably across the paths that could lead us toward a better future. But worse than they, I think, are the majority of members of both houses who continue to submit to the senility system. Apparently, they hope they, too, will grow to be old.

Many of the men in Congress are not their own bosses. A little observation of each of them, a very little sometimes, is all one needs to see who plays the tune to which he dances. Not owning themselves, they cannot be independent. They cannot risk losing the friends and favors they have built up, which makes them valuable enough to be salable to the interest groups who back them. I have often had men say, in my presence, with a wry face, "Well, I voted wrong on that one." "Why?" I have asked, and the answer is "Well . . . politics."

It is likely I won't last as long in Congress as some of them; I have had a feeling all along that I will probably do my thing for six or eight years at most, and then somehow my refusal to compromise will catch up with me. But I am not only concerned about being in the House for twenty years. Sometime somebody has to start trying to change things, start to say something, do something, be politically expendable. My little rebellion was not intended to sink the system; I was simply mad at being put where I would be wasted, and I could not keep quiet about it.

Some of the Washington press corps clucked over my actions and waited for the thunderbolts to vaporize me. So far it hasn't happened, although it still may; politicians have long memories for a slight or challenge and can wait a long time to even things. Those are the rules of the game.

At the next Democratic caucus, I was assigned to the Veterans' Affairs Committee, whose chairman, Olin "Tiger" Teague of Texas, had assured me after the first caucus that he would be delighted to have me on his committee anytime. It was an improvement; as I told people, "There are a lot more veterans in my district than there are trees."

The pleasant surprise was the editorial support I got — not from the sophisticated capital press, but from many other papers, including the country's largest, the *New York Daily News,* which said I showed courage, was right, and might even help "put an end to the boobery that exiles urban lawmakers to such committees while representatives from the hay-and-hog circuit grapple with city-bred problems of slums, poverty and education beyond their ken."

A suburban paper, the Rockland County *Journal News,* also got my point: "Mrs. Chisholm was not knocking the Agriculture Committee . . . nor was she contending that freshmen should have the undiluted right to demand this or that committee assignment . . . The point is that seniority is a defensible criterion in making committee assignments, but should not be the sole or the paramount consideration. A legislator's background, interests and attitudes should count for something, too, as should the nature and predominant concerns of the district he or she has been elected to represent — and to help."

Tiger Teague followed up his invitation to be on his Veterans' Affairs Committee with messages offering to put me on the education and training subcommittees. He was the one committee chairman who offered me a place. I don't know how the leadership decided where to put me, but probably the reasoning was "If Tiger wants her, let him have her." I heard by the grapevine that the leadership expected me to do the same kind of thing again. The House was bothered about me from the time I got there because the media were painting me as a nonconformist and they had no idea what I was going to do next.

Some of the reporters who have been covering Congress so long that, chameleonlike, they think like congressmen, have been outraged at me ever since. One wire service writer wrote a piece lecturing me about how naive I had been. "Power and influence in Congress," he explained, "are not obtained by promoting one's own measures. They come either from blocking measures others want enacted or supporting measures others oppose. As a member of the Agriculture Committee, Mrs. Chisholm would have been in an ideal position to make her presence felt. Without offending her own constituents, she could have voted against all of the bills introduced for the benefit of farmers. At the same time she could have introduced bills to scuttle price supports and other farm programs. Before long, farm belt congressmen would have been knocking on her door, asking favors."

That kind of long-range Machiavellian strategy may be fine for a white, midwestern congressman whose district has more cows than voters, and who has all the time in the world to try to work himself up to that comfortable share of power that a House member can achieve if he plays by the rules, makes his district "safe," and lives long enough. What I can never forget, and what my friend the reporter apparently never knew, is that there are children in my district who will not live long enough for me to play it the way he proposes.

The question is what kind of a role I should play as a black member of Congress at this point in the historic struggle. The temptations are many. I could try to represent all the blacks in the country and work to cure the evils of 200 years immediately. As I pointed out in the caucus speech refusing the committee assignment, there are only nine black members of the House, although, with 15 percent of the population, black Americans should have far more representation — perhaps fifty-five members would be about fair. None of us in the nine can be equal to the impossible burden of responsibility. Each of us must do what he can. I represent an urban constituency beset with problems of housing, employment, and education. I must voice its needs. How?

Not as a legislator. Even if he is not black and not a member of the smallest faction in the House, the left-liberal one, a freshman member is not going to get many — if any —

laws passed. He has no clout. No one cares what he does; the business of the House goes on with or without him. What then should be my role?

It seems to me that the most important things I can do are to, first, use my position to help people who elected me in practical ways. My "case load" — the Capitol Hill phrase for the problems that people bring to their representatives, covering everything from discrimination in employment to unjust imprisonment — must be one of the heaviest on the Hill. If I can, I help black Americans whether they are from my district or not. I have to concentrate on my district, of course, because those are the people who elected me and who have first claim on my services, and also because there may be no other place in the nation where there are so many critical human problems needing help. But there are so many black, brown, yellow, red, and poor white Americans who can hope for little help from their own elected representatives that it is only natural that some of them come to those of us from whom they can hope for a little human sympathy and concern. The nine black members present all feel the pressure that results from this.

Second, I can use my office to apply pressure to the federal machinery to try to save programs and get new ones, to secure grants for my district, and to fight discrimination on federal contracts. It has been estimated that one third of all the jobs in the country are covered by laws forbidding discrimination because federal money is involved, either in direct federal employment, buying through contracts, or in grants or loans, such as for highways and schools. These laws are not being enforced. The record of federal agencies, particularly of the Defense Department, is nauseating in this regard. The housing laws, the equal employment opportunity laws, many more laws that are already on the books are not being used. We don't need any more legislation for a while. What we need is a Congress — and an administration — that will permit the ones we have to work. At present we have neither; we have, in fact, just the opposite.

So I do not see myself as a lawmaker, an innovator in the field of legislation. America has the laws and the material resources it takes to insure justice for all its people. What it lacks is the heart, the humanity, the Christian love that it would take. It is perhaps unrealistic to hope that I can help give this nation any of those things, but that is what I believe I have to try to do.

Part III

Speaking Out

9

The Speech Against the War

THE MONTH I ENTERED CONGRESS, January 1968, the Nixon administration came into office, bearing a heavy load of hope, including the hopes of black Americans. During the campaign, the new President had said, "If our cities are to be livable for the next generation, we can delay no longer in launching new approaches to the problems that beset them and to the tensions that tear them apart . . ." And he said, "When you cut expenditures for education, what you are doing is shortchanging the American future."

Well, it sounded right. During the first months of the new administration, many of us waited for action to suit the words. We who had not supported Richard Nixon could not have been expected to be optimistic, but we suspended disbelief and waited to see what the new administration would do.

Among those who were waiting was Allard Lowenstein, who was elected with me. He had run for the House on Long Island after some two years of intensive leadership of the peace campaign. Lowenstein, who had organized the anti-Johnson campaign that came to be headed by Senator

Eugene McCarthy, was notably silent on the subject of the war for his first seven months in office. He was deliberately keeping his peace, on the principle that the new President deserved every chance to show whether his new perspectives and lack of responsibility for the mistakes of the past would achieve the goals that we and, we believed, a majority of Americans wanted: a quick end to the unjust war we had drifted into, and a redirection of our national wealth and energy to the attack on hunger, poverty, ignorance, and the other evils that flourish in this country. It was not until nearly fall that Al Lowenstein broke his silence, after a trip to Vietnam had showed him that the President's claims that we were withdrawing troops and winding down the war were belied by the facts. I lost my optimism much earlier.

By the end of March, these events among others had taken place: the Secretary of Commerce, Maurice Stans, had confided to a reporter that the new administration was pretty well agreed it had to take time out from major social objectives until it could stop inflation. The Secretary of Health, Education, and Welfare at the time, Robert Finch, had testified that the country ought to be spending more on education, particularly in city schools, but it just couldn't afford to until it reached some kind of honorable solution to the Vietnam war. The Secretary of Defense, Melvin Laird, came to Capitol Hill to persuade the Senate to build an antiballistic missile system, and to read his testimony one would have thought it was former Secretary of State Dean Rusk talking. He spoke of being prepared to spend at least two more years in Vietnam.

Now, I am not a pacifist. Ending the war had not been a major theme of my campaign; it was ninth on a list of nine goals that I had pledged to fight for if I were elected, behind jobs, job training, equality education, adequate housing, enforcement of antidiscrimination laws, support for day care centers, and several other items. But when President Nixon announced, on the same day, that he had decided that the United States would not be safe until we started to build an ABM system, and that the Head Start program in the District of Columbia was to be cut back for lack of money, that was enough for me. I started working on my maiden speech in the House. For whatever it would be worth, even if it would only get it off my chest, I had to tell the world that it was wrong to plan to spend billions on an elaborate and unnecessary weapons system when disadvantaged children were getting nothing.

The juxtaposition of the two presidential announcements was the theme of my speech, but there were dozens of other indications of the administration's intentions that I could have seized on. Nor was the bias in favor of weapons of death and against programs for peace all at the White House end of Pennsylvania Avenue. There was the case of Pride, Incorporated. This is a vigorous and successful black organization that grew up spontaneously among young men in the inner city of the District of Columbia. Originally its program was to kill rats and clean up litter; it was so successful that it earned a million-dollar federal grant to continue its program and expand into new fields, particularly the creation of jobs for young, unemployed black men. Its enemies on the Hill turned a team of at least six auditors from the General Accounting Office loose on Pride. They worked seven months and spent more than $100,000. At last they reported they had uncovered a fraud — it involved a little less than $2100. In the same seven months billions of dollars were spent by the Department of Defense. How many auditors were checking up on the cozy, classified, negotiated contracts on which the billions were spent? Just five.

But more important was the contrast that was so plain to me that I could not understand why it was not plain to everyone, including the other members of Congress. While we gave the military a blank check to dream up new weapons, following up revelations of their worthlessness and wastefulness with decisions to spend more on them, we were merciless with the failures of social programs. Take the Job Corps. Its shortcomings and mistakes were criticized at length, although the amounts involved were trivial compared to military spending waste. Its accomplishments were greater than its failures, and its promise greater still. If it had been a research and development program creating better ways to kill, it would have been pronounced invaluable, and billions would have been poured into it.

It seemed to me that there was only one possible course for me to take. I could not vote for money for war while funds were being denied to feed, house, and school Americans. There was no way to be selective about it. I could not vote yes on funds for defense and no on funds for the Vietnam war or any similar misadventures. When an appropriations bill comes to a vote in Congress, it is all or nothing; all an individual member can do is swallow the whole thing and vote yes, or reject it in its entirety. As I said, I am not a pacifist. Our country must be ready to protect itself when necessary, and its citizens must be ready to give their lives for it, in a just and unavoidable conflict. The war in Southeast Asia was neither just nor unavoidable; it was an unnecessary war into which we stumbled, led by shortsighted, stubborn men who could not admit at any point that they were wrong but who, on the contrary, concealed their mistakes by systematically lying to the country about the nature of the war and the prospects of ending it.

"We Americans," I said in my maiden speech late in March,

"have come to feel that it is our mission to make the world free. We believe that we are the good guys, everywhere, in Vietnam, in Latin America, wherever we go. We believe we are good guys at home, too. When the Kerner Commission told white America what black America has always known, that prejudice and hatred built the nation's slums, maintains them and profits by them, white America could not believe it. But it is true. Unless we start to fight and defeat the enemies in our own country, poverty and racism, and make our talk of equality and opportunity ring true, we are exposed in the eyes of the world as hypocrites when we talk about making people free.

"I am deeply disappointed at the clear evidence that the number one priority of the new administration is to buy more and more and more weapons of war, to return to the era of the Cold War and to ignore the war we must fight here, the war that is not optional. There is only one way, I believe, to turn these policies around. The Congress must respond to the mandate that the American people have clearly expressed. They have said, 'End this war. Stop the waste. Stop the killing. Do something for our own people first.' . . ."

I concluded, "We must force the administration to rethink its distorted, unreal scale of priorities. Our children, our jobless men, our deprived, rejected, and starving fellow citizens must come first. For this reason, I intend to vote 'no' on every money bill that comes to the floor of this House that provides any funds for the Department of Defense. Any bill whatsoever, until the time comes when our values and priorities have been turned right-side up again, until the monstrous waste and the shocking profits in the defense budget have been eliminated and our country starts to use its strength, its tremendous resources, for people and peace, not for profits and war."

In a movie, of course, the House would have given me a standing ovation and members would have crowded around to congratulate me and confess that they understood for the first time what was happening and were behind me from then on. But the reality of Congress is that no one is usually swayed one way or another by any speech made on the floor. Debate in the House is not discussion, give-and-take to clarify the issues, an attempt to make up other members' minds. It is a succession of monologues in which everyone gets his predetermined stand on the record. Sometimes it is like a poker game, in which each side reveals some of the strength it has, trying to make it just enough to convince a waverer that there is a lot more being held back and he'd better join the winning side. It is seldom that anyone listens to what is being said on the floor of the House.

All that happened was that as I walked out I overheard (probably I was meant to overhear) one member say to another, "You know, she's crazy!" Later other colleagues told me that even if I really believed what I had said, it was not a wise political move to say so publicly. After all, the country was at war and responsible congressional leaders shouldn't say they are not going to support defense bills. Think of the soldiers over there: how do they feel when they read that the country isn't behind them and that some people are talking about not supporting them even with the material they need to stay alive?

Only a handful of members of Congress dared to defy such logic — at most twenty of us. You can't argue with someone whose premises are completely different from yours, where there is not even an inch of common ground. What I wanted was perfectly plain. It was not to deny support to servicemen in Vietnam, for heaven's sake, but to bring them home at once, to stop forcing them to risk death or disfigurement in the defense of a corrupt puppet dictatorship. What I saw was this country at war with itself, and no one in a position of power paying any attention, our lives deteriorating around us and scarcely anyone trying to find out why and stop it.

It was after that that student groups began to pay attention to me. Apparently the sharp language in my speech against the war struck a responsive chord. Not many older persons were verbalizing students' sentiments, even if they shared them, as clearly and unequivocally as I happened to do. I began to be drowned in requests to speak on campuses. It was impossible to do more than acknowledge most of them, but I told my staff to arrange for me to fill as many as possible, even at the expense of more lucrative and politically advantageous appearances.

10

How I View Congress

A NEW CONGRESSMAN faces a lot of disappointments. One most freshman House members share is the discovery that, while getting elected made him a big man back home, Washington has seen green representatives arrive by the thousands and is not very impressed.

Then, unless he has had legislative experience, he will be frustrated to learn that his plans for laws that will solve the problems of the country, whatever he sees them to be, are doomed because he is a very junior member of a rather large group. It was a little less frustrating for me because my terms in the New York State Assembly had wised me up about what could and could not be done through the legislative process as it works at present.

I also stood out from the crowd at first, at least to the news media. While this would delight many members, I was not very happy about it. Requests for interviews flooded into my office in the early weeks and so did invitations to dinners and parties. I gave as many interviews as I could, but even if I had spent all of my time with the press it would not have satisfied them. As for the parties, I knew from the start that the Washington social whirl was not for me. In Albany and New York, I had seen the political party circuit. I stayed away from it in those places and I came to Washington determined to do the same thing. Quite a few people think I'm aloof and antisocial. Actually I'm gregarious, but I am selective about whom I want to be with. The cocktail and dinner party circuit is mostly made up of hangers-on, dealers, and self-promoters. The people who really do things are not party people. They have too little free time to spend it at parties listening to people who are glassy eyed with alcohol and making little sense. My weekly routine, like that of most members of Congress who are within traveling distance of their home districts, is to spend four long days in the capital and three longer ones back home. I leave my office as a rule no earlier than 7:30 in the evening, later when a House session runs late. Occasionally I have a speaking engagement in the Washington area, and more rarely a television show to tape; unless there is some such obligation to discharge, I go home, have dinner, and get in bed with the memorandums, reports, and letters I will have to know about the next day. On Thursday evenings, unless there is a Friday session of the House (there seldom is unless Congress is bearing down to clear up its work for adjournment), I fly back to Brooklyn. The three-day weekends are not a time for rest. At least one full day is spent in my district office. On top of that, I have a heavy speaking schedule, taking me to all parts of the country. Nearly every Sunday morning, I appear as the speaker at some church. It's a good thing I'm *not* a party type, because I just don't have the time for it.

Of course, not all House members feel that way, and there are some, even in key jobs, who could be described politely as inebriates. Their identities are well known to their colleagues, but it is bad manners to name them "outside the family." If an unwary wino or even a tourist is caught on the Capitol grounds with an open bottle, the police will chase him away or arrest him. That law isn't enforced against members of Congress. Especially just before a session adjourns, when the days on the floor get long, one begins to notice the traffic in and out of the side doors of the House chamber, to the cloakrooms. Before long, there are red faces and unsteady gaits. If that were the worst failing of Congress, though, we would have little to worry about. The weakness of a few members for the sauce is no big thing.

Something more shocking is the way members come panting into the chamber after the bells ring for a roll call vote and ask a colleague, perhaps the first one they see, "How are we going on this?" If the second member says, "We're going aye on this," the first man goes and votes aye. The practice is common, but it always shocks me. Some members are sorry later, when they find out the effect of their votes.

The attitudes some members of Congress display toward the rest of humanity, including their constituents, sometimes irritates and sometimes dismays me. They act like aristocrats. It has been a long time since Thomas Jefferson was sworn in as President, then rode his horse back to a boardinghouse and sat down to dinner with the rest of the roomers. Now even the most junior member of the House is surrounded by a hush of deference when he moves around the Hill. When the bells announce a roll call vote, citizens are kept off the elevators so he can rush over to the floor. Two other members and I boarded an elevator once, on our way to a roll call, as a group of young people were about to get on. One of the other congressmen blocked their way. "You can't get on this elevator," he said. "Why not?" a girl asked. "You just can't come on here now," he replied, and snapped at the elevator operator, "Let's get going." The contempt with which he spoke and looked at the youngsters was amazing. I was proud of the kids; they just laughed. (On the Senate side of the Hill, it is even worse; many of the elevators are reserved for Senators only throughout the day.)

I have overheard members talking with groups that have come to see them, telling them how glad they are to have them, how nice that they came all the way to Washington. Then, the delegation gone, they will remark to a colleague, "I hope that bunch doesn't come back in a hurry." Some members of Congress are among the best actors in the world.

It was more than a year before I realized that there is one section of the spectators' gallery for women and one for men. Such fossil practices are everywhere one looks in the Congress. A girl applied recently for a job as a page and was turned down, although she was perfectly qualified. While I'm not sure I'd want a daughter of mine to associate with some congressmen, such horse-and-buggy thinking has got to be changed.

But these are only symptoms of the basic problem, a problem that can wreck our nation if it is not solved. Our representative democracy is not working because the Congress that is supposed to represent the voters does not respond to their needs. I believe the chief reason is that it is ruled by a small group of old men. The majority of members of the House have surrendered their power to a tiny minority — the Speaker, the party organization leaders, and the chairmen of the committees. They could take it back at any time, but apparently they are afraid to.

Congress has to have leaders, and it would be paralyzed without its committee system. The trouble lies with the way leaders and chairmen are chosen, particularly the chairmen. They rise by seniority. Nothing else matters — competence, character, past performance, background, or orientation. All a man has to do is stay alive and keep getting reelected, and he will be a power in Washington in twenty or thirty years. He may be from a rural backwater. The odds are that he will be, because the "safe districts" are generally that kind. He may be a reactionary, a bigot, a mediocrity. The odds are that he will be, if nothing worse, a man of narrow outlook and modest endowments, because a man of that caliber is the kind who will be satisfied to stay in the House and do nothing for decades that would risk his chances of reelection.

So our troubled, embattled, urban society, looking to Washington for wisdom and help, finds that the processes of change are thwarted by the control of old men whose values are those of a small-town lawyer or a feed-store operator. If they react at all to the challenge of our age, it is with incomprehension and irritation. Congress seems drugged and inert most of the time. Even when the problems it ignores build up to crises and erupt in strikes, riots, and demonstrations, it is not moved. Its idea of meeting a problem is to hold hearings or, in extreme cases, to appoint a commission.

Most congressional hearings are ridiculous. They are held to impress the public, to get someone's name in the papers and on television. Up at the front of the room, the committee sits high on a dais behind a mahogany counter and the lowly masses sit out front. Witnesses come in and earnestly testify about something they know and care about, hoping that the committee will be moved. They think if they give Congress the truth, they will get justice in return. Then their testimony is printed in book after book of hearing records, which are piled on shelves to gather dust. When the clamor becomes loud enough on some issue, Congress will grumble in its doze and pass some patchwork legislation designed to irritate as few people as possible.

To consider the money spent on hearings, committees,

commissions, studies, and trips and think what else it could be used for is depressing. Early in 1970, I voted no on a measure to pay for a trip to Asia by members of the Education and Labor Committee, a little pleasure jaunt to wile away a recess. Even some of the black committee members were hurt. They looked at me as if to ask, "Shirley, why don't you want us to go on a little trip?" It wasn't a great deal of money. But it might better have been spent on one city day care center's operation, or one rural public health team — things the members of that committee are supposed to care about. There are American children whose bellies are distended with tapeworms, who are crippled by malnutrition. How could we vote money for that trip? I was angry, while they were angry at me.

Each year educators, businessmen, labor leaders, and all sorts of others come to Washington and trek the halls of Congress anxiously trying to find out when and how action will be taken on appropriations bills that they depend on. Each year state governments are hobbled when they make up their budgets because Congress has not acted on money bills and they don't know what to count on. To stall a little longer, Congress passes "continuing resolutions," which keep money going out at last year's spending level. Then the talk goes on, and nothing happens, and more continuing resolutions are passed. It is inexcusable, because the House has to handle the same appropriations bills every year. Everyone knows from the start of a session what has to be done. But it is not done for months, and then it is done badly. Afterward, the leaders of both parties get on the floor and blame each other.

Maybe, in addition to their other faults, the old men just can't work fast enough. If so, they ought to step back and give the young a chance. Probably the age of congressmen should be limited to sixty-five. Six or eight terms in the House or three or four in the Senate should be the limit regardless of age. The committee system should be shaken up, with members being moved around more. When they stay on one committee forever, they tend to be corrupted by their contact with special interest representatives, who court them for their influence.

Conflicts of interest should be grounds for impeachment. Banking and Currency Committee members now are allowed to be directors of banks — a shocking state of affairs. The best way to ensure that this cannot happen is to require complete financial disclosure by members of Congress. Everything they earn and every business or professional connection they keep should be fully public. As things are now, no one can tell to whom members of Congress are responsible, except that it does not often appear to be to the people. Everyone else is represented in Washington by a rich and powerful lobby, it seems. But there is no lobby for the people.

When I first came to Washington, I would sometimes confide to other members how I wanted to help the people of my community. It became embarrassing. I was talking a foreign language to some of my colleagues when I said "community" and "people." Of course, there are members of whom that is not true. Some fine men are in Congress, too few, trying to do a responsible job. But they are surrounded and almost neutralized by a greater number whose instinct is to make a deal before they make a decision.

Some of the latter have tried to educate me. They told me that this is part of the business I hadn't learned. "You trade," one said to me. "You don't give your vote away for nothing." Trade the trust of the people who elected them for personal advantage? This cynicism is so pervasive that even men who start out honest can succumb to it without realizing. Even if

that doesn't happen, they can become passive out of disillu-
sionment and drift with the currents. Why bruise your head
against a wall?

Almost every week I see busloads of people who come from
all over to work for legislation they want and need. They go
through a routine of getting lists of members' names, divid-
ing into groups, and calling on congressmen. Sometimes they
get an audience, sometimes they have to settle for talking to
a staff assistant. But after they leave, nothing has changed.
Their efforts do not show in the way the votes are cast. Who
is it that Congress represents? Would things be different if
citizens were more highly organized and better able to artic-
ulate and emphasize their desires? This is a serious problem
that has to be solved if the democratic process is going to
work in a nation as large and complex as ours. As it is now,
Congress is just making believe. It is going through motions
to make the voters think a democratic process is going on.
The trouble is the voters are growing too sophisticated to believe it much longer.

One unexpected disappointment for me was a group that
I expected to embody the best in the House, the "liberal
bloc" organization called the Democratic Study Group. The
DSG should be a progressive element, leading the way toward
change, fighting for forward-looking legislation. But it seems
to have too short an attention span. Time after time I saw
it become enthusiastic about some issue, only to have its
troops fall out of line halfway to the fight. The DSG talks a
good game, but it lacks conviction. It never seems to get
together and do anything. It is a somewhat nebulous organization in its size. If the issue is not too hot, it can count well
over 100 votes on its side. But when the pressure is on and a
real matter of principle is involved, its strength will dwindle
to twenty or thirty. For instance, in 1969 when it was a ques-

tion of making the only meaningful attack on the continuation of the Vietnam war that is within the House's power — by denying money to keep it going — the DSG took no stand. There were twenty-one no votes. The rest found that their antiwar convictions were not strong enough, after all, to require them to take the risk of voting that way.

The liberals in the House strongly resemble liberals I have known through the last two decades in the civil rights conflict. When it comes time to show on which side they will be counted, they suddenly excuse themselves. Black people have come to expect this kind of betrayal. As an example, there was a time when open housing committees were fashionable in the New York City area, making an effort to pry open the barriers of bigotry that confine black and brown Americans to the city slums. Some of my liberal friends were on these committees. One suburban woman I knew well was president of a housing conference, ostensibly trying to integrate her community. Her husband, a realtor, was on a real estate men's board that was protesting against "flooding" the area with "certain kinds of people." My friend's efforts for the cause were, you can imagine, quite feeble.

When morality comes up against profit, it is seldom that profit loses. The liberal civil rights campaigners in the suburbs usually shied away when they were asked to take a firm stand that might make someone else angry, and the excuse they gave was, all too often, "We have to do business with these people." It has begun to occur to me that liberals in Congress are not very different. They say all the right things, their hearts are in the right place, but they keep trying to do things without ever actually doing anything. Without a deeper and more sincere commitment by some of its members, it will never be possible to get enough bodies and minds together to make the Congress of the United States more relevant to the times and meaningful to its constituents.

White politicians and political analysts started watching at the opening of the 91st Congress to see who was going to wind up the leader of the "black bloc." No one did, and they sometimes showed themselves puzzled by this. With nine black members of the House (a tenth black is in the Senate), the largest number since Reconstruction, we were expected to form a "bloc" and act as a unified force. It was the same kind of naiveté that has led white politicians and journalists to look for a "leader" in each black community — once they had made the belated discovery that a black community exists. This state of mind among whites has resulted, as is becoming better known, in some very odd self-appointed "leaders" being singled out by whites and courted enthusiastically. Often those same "leaders" are and always were objects of ridicule or suspicion to most of the black citizens they pretend to speak for.

The nine black members of the House are nine different human beings, of different ages and backgrounds, different interests and dispositions, and from different kinds of communities. With the intense pressures on us, from our own people and from the rest of the country, jealousies and rivalries have been aroused. I suppose that was inevitable. At an earlier time, there was no problem because Adam Clayton Powell was clearly the boss black congressman. But his **star** has declined and does not look likely to rise again. Who will be his successor?

Probably no one. I hope there will be none. At meetings of the "black delegation" — and we do meet, more than most people know — I have said, "Who needs a leader for nine people?" We each have our individual strengths. Some of us, like me, are talkers, persuaders, preachers. Others can work with other members of Congress, even conservative whites, in a way that I cannot. Others are researchers, creators, organizers. There is a danger that we will fall into the trap of not cooperating for fear of projecting one member into the limelight to the dismay of the others. Certainly I do not want that one to be me. I do not want to be the "black leader" in the House. Unfortunately, because I have national recognition thanks to the accident of being the only black woman member, at press conferences the television cameras and reporters seldom fail to cluster around me. I have seen the unhappy looks on the other members' faces when this happens, and one result is that I have sometimes ducked meetings with the media in order to stay more in the background.

At least once, I was able to see what the impact could be if the "black bloc" could overcome its divisions and work together. In September 1969, when Representative John Conyers of Detroit testified in behalf of the black members against the nomination of Judge Clement Haynesworth to the Supreme Court, most of us went in a body to listen and show our support. It seemed to me that the effect was visible. Whether we changed any votes, we will never know. But I believe we left our mark.

It was during the Haynesworth affair that I most clearly saw racism at work in the Congress. I couldn't believe much of what I heard in the debates and saw in the Senate hearing room. The contempt that radiated from some of the Judiciary Committee toward anti-Haynesworth witnesses like Clarence Mitchell of the NAACP was astonishing. When he came in, most of the members sat back — perhaps the single exception was Senator Birch Bayh — with their posture proclaiming their reaction: "Well, here he is again." They asked a few mechanical questions and hardly listened to the answers.

During the House debate on the extension of the Voting Rights Act, the essentially racist nature of the question was kept in the background. It was fascinating to hear some of the southern members argue their case. They were so subtle that, unless you knew what they were up to, you could almost believe they meant it when they said that, after all, the act should be extended to all the states — with just a few little changes, of course. "It should be not only for all the nigras in the South but for everybody," one white brother said piously.

Sometimes southern members stop to talk to me, and I feel they wish they had a knife to open me up down the middle and see what's inside. I know they think, as many people do, that I don't understand politics. I understand it too damned well, after all my years in it, and that's why I want to change it. I did not come to Congress to behave myself and stay away from explosive issues so I can keep coming back. Under the circumstances, it's hard for me to imagine I will stay here long. There isn't much that I can do inside Congress in a legislative way. There is a great deal I can do for the people of my district by using my office and the resources it opens up to me in helping individuals and groups. I can investigate the unfair treatment of a black sergeant in the air force, and I can help a black businessman in Brooklyn apply for a Small Business Administration loan, and do so successfully in a satisfying number of cases. This kind of work is important, and it occupies a lot of my time and most of the time of my staff.

But beyond that, my most valuable function, I think, is as a voice. The accident of my prominence at this period in the struggle of my race for justice and equality can be a good thing if I use it well. I work to be a major force for change outside the House, even if I cannot be one within it. I still believe that our system of representative government can work. It deserves another chance. I feel change will come, sooner or later. It has to, because of the young people and their insistence that things be made better. Whether we love them or curse them, their ideals and their tactics on the campuses and in the streets are forcing the nation out of its lethargy. They will make us move whether we want to or not. If my hopes fail, I'll have to seek another course. I have already moved away from being a moderate, a liberal. My frustrations at trying to operate through channels and following the prescribed procedures, and failing to get any action, have radicalized me. But I don't think yet that our society is doomed. It could be, if the inertia of the majority of our citizens, induced by their incredibly high standard of living, continues.

Most Americans have never seen the ignorance, degradation, hunger, sickness, and futility in which many other Americans live. Until a problem reaches their doorsteps, they're not going to understand. They won't become involved in economic or political change until something brings the seriousness of the situation home to them. Until they are threatened, why should they change a system that has been fairly beneficial for a fairly large number of people? It is going to have to be the have-nots — the blacks, browns, reds, yellows, and whites who do not share in the good life that most Americans lead — who somehow arouse the conscience of the nation and thus create a conscience in the Congress. My role, as I see it, is to help them do so, working outside of Washington, perhaps, as much as inside it.

11

Facing the Abortion Question

I N AUGUST OF 1969 I started to get phone calls from NARAL, the National Association for the Repeal of Abortion Laws, a new organization based in New York City that was looking for a national president. In the New York State Assembly I had supported abortion reform bills introduced by Assemblyman Albert Blumenthal, and this had apparently led NARAL to believe I would sympathize with its goal: complete repeal of all laws restricting abortion. As a matter of fact, when I was in the Assembly I had not been in favor of repealing all abortion laws, a step that would leave the question of having or not having the operation entirely up to a woman and her doctor. The bills I had tried to help pass in Albany would only have made it somewhat easier for women to get therapeutic abortions in New York State, by providing additional legal grounds and simplifying the procedure for getting approval. But since that time I had been compelled to do some heavy thinking on the subject, mainly because of the experiences of several young women I knew. All had suffered permanent injuries at the hands of illegal abortionists. Some will never have children as a result. One will have to go to a hospital periodically for treatment for the rest of her life.

It had begun to seem to me that the question was not whether the law should allow abortions. Experience shows that pregnant women who feel they have compelling reasons for not having a baby, or another baby, will break the law and, even worse, risk injury and death if they must to get one. Abortions will not be stopped. It may even be that the number performed is not being greatly reduced by laws making an abortion a "criminal operation." If that is true, the question becomes simply that of what kind of abortions society wants women to have — clean, competent ones performed by licensed physicians or septic, dangerous ones done by incompetent practitioners.

So when NARAL asked me to lead its campaign, I gave it serious thought. For me to take the lead in abortion repeal would be an even more serious step than for a white politician to do so, because there is a deep and angry suspicion among many blacks that even birth control clinics are a plot by the white power structure to keep down the numbers of blacks, and this opinion is even more strongly held by some in regard to legalizing abortions. But I do not know any black or Puerto Rican *women* who feel that way. To label family planning and legal abortion programs "genocide" is male rhetoric, for male ears. It falls flat to female listeners, and to thoughtful male ones. Women know, and so do many men, that two or three children who are wanted, prepared for, reared amid love and stability, and educated to the limit of their ability will mean more for the future of the black and brown races from which they come than any number of neglected, hungry, ill-housed and ill-clothed youngsters. Pride in one's race, as well as simple humanity, supports this view. Poor women of every race feel as I do, I believe. There is objective evidence of it in a study by Dr. Charles F. Westhoff of the Princeton Office of Population Research. He questioned 5600 married persons and found that 22 percent of their children were unwanted. But among persons who earn less than $4000 a year, 42 percent of the children were unwanted. The poor are more anxious about family planning than any other group.

Why then do the poor keep on having large families? It is not because they are stupid or immoral. One must understand how many resources their poverty has deprived them of, and that chief among these is medical care and advice. The poor do not go to doctors or clinics except when they absolutely must; their medical ignorance is very great, even when compared to the low level of medical knowledge most persons have. This includes, naturally, information about contraceptives and how to get them. In some of the largest cities, clinics are now attacking this problem; they are nowhere near to solving it. In smaller cities and in most of the countryside, hardly anything is being done.

Another point is this: not only do the poor have large families, but also large families tend to be poor. More than one fourth of all the families with four children live in poverty, according to the federal government's excessively narrow definition; by humane standards of poverty, the number would be much larger. The figures range from 9 percent of one-child families that have incomes below the official poverty line, up to 42 percent of the families with six children or more. Sinking into poverty, large families tend to stay there because of the educational and social handicaps that being poor imposes. It is the fear of such a future for their children that drives many women, of every color and social stratum, except perhaps the highest, to seek abortions when contraception has failed.

Botched abortions are the largest single cause of death of pregnant women in the United States, particularly among nonwhite women. In 1964, the president of the New York County Medical Society, Dr. Carl Goldmark, estimated that 80 percent of the deaths of gravid women in Manhattan were from this cause.

Another study by Edwin M. Gold, covering 1960 through 1962, gave lower percentages but supplied evidence that women from minority groups suffer most. Gold said abortion was the cause of death in 25 percent of the white cases, 49 percent of the black ones, and 65 percent of the Puerto Rican ones.

Even when a poor woman needs an abortion for the most impeccable medical reasons, acceptable under most states' laws, she is not likely to succeed in getting one. The public hospitals to which she must go are far more reluctant to approve abortions than are private, voluntary hospitals. It's in the records: private hospitals in New York City perform 3.9 abortions for every 1000 babies they deliver, public hospitals only 1 per 1000. Another relevant figure is that 90 percent of the therapeutic abortions in the city are performed on white women. Such statistics convinced me that my instinctive feeling was right: a black woman legislator, far from avoiding the abortion question, was compelled to face it and deal with it.

But my time did not permit me to be an active president of NARAL, so I asked to be made an honorary president. My appearances on television in September 1969, when the association's formation was announced, touched off one of the heaviest flows of mail to my Washington office that I have experienced. What surprised me was that it was overwhelmingly in favor of repeal. Most of the letters that disagreed with me were from Catholics, and most of them were temperate and reasoned. We sent those writers a reply that said in part, "No one should be forced to have an abortion or to use birth control methods which for religious or personal reasons they oppose. But neither should others who have different views be forced to abide by what they do not and cannot believe in." Some of the mail was from desperate women who thought I could help them. "I am forty-five years old," one wrote, "and have raised a family already. Now I find that I am pregnant and I need help. Please send me all the information." A girl wrote that she was pregnant and did not dare tell her mother and stepfather: "Please send me the name of a doctor or hospital that would help. You said if my doctor wouldn't do it to write to you. Where can I turn?" We sent the writers of these letters a list of the names and addresses of the chapters of the Clergy Consultation Service on Abortion and suggested that they find a local family planning or birth control clinic.

The reaction of a number of my fellow members of Congress seemed to me a little strange. Several said to me, "This abortion business . . . my God, what are you doing? That's not politically wise." It was the same old story; they were not thinking in terms of right or wrong, they were considering only whether taking a side of the issue would help them stay in office — or in this case, whether taking a stand would help me get reelected. They concluded that it would not help me, so it was a bad position for me to take. My advisers were, of course, all men. So I decided to shake them up a little with a feminist line of counterattack. "Who told you I shouldn't do this?" I asked them. "Women are dying every day, did you know that? They're being butchered and maimed. No matter what men think, abortion is a fact of life. Women will have them; they always have and always will. Are they going to have good ones or bad ones? Will the good ones be reserved for the rich while poor women have to go to quacks?

Why don't we talk about real problems instead of phony ones?"

One member asked the question that was on the minds of all the others: "How many Catholics do you have in your district?" "Look," I told him, "I can't worry about that. That's not the problem." Persons who do not deal with politicians are often baffled by the peculiarly simple workings of their minds. Scientists and scholars in particular are bewildered by the political approach. When a member of Congress makes a statement, the scholar's first thought is "Is what he said true? Is he right or wrong?" The falseness or validity of an officeholder's statement is almost never discussed in Washington, or anyplace where politics sets the tone of discourse. The question political people ask is seldom "Is he right?" but "Why did he say that?" Or they ask, "Where does he expect that to get him?" or "Who put him up to that?"

But returning to abortion, the problem that faced me was what action I should take in my role as a legislator, if any; naturally, I intended to be as active as possible as an advocate and publicist for the cause, but was there any chance of getting a meaningful bill through Congress? Some NARAL officials wanted me to introduce an abortion repeal bill as a gesture. This is very common; probably a majority of the bills introduced in all legislative bodies are put in for the sake of effect, to give their sponsor something to talk about on the stump. That was never my style in Albany, and I have not adopted it in Washington. When I introduce legislation, I try to draft it carefully and then look for meaningful support from people who have the power to help move the bill.

So I looked for House members, in both parties and of all shades of conservatism and liberalism, who might get together on abortion repeal regardless of party. I wrote letters to a number of the more influential House members. It would have been easy to get three or four, or even ten or twelve, liberal Democrats to join me in introducing a bill, but nothing would have happened. A majority of House members would have said, "Oh, that bunch again," and dismissed us. But just a few conservative Republican co-sponsors, or conservative Democratic ones, would change all that. The approach I took was eminently sound, but it didn't work. A few members replied that they would support my bill if it ever got to the floor, but could not come out for it publicly before then or work for it. I did not doubt their sincerity, but it was a safe thing to say because the chances of a bill's reaching the floor seemed slim. Several others answered with longish letters admiring my bold position and expressing sympathy, but not agreement. "I am not ready to assume such a position," one letter said. Another said, in almost these words, "This kind of trouble I don't need." So I put my roughly drafted bill in a drawer and decided to wait. There is no point in introducing it until congressmen can be persuaded to vote for it, and only one thing will persuade them. If a congressman feels he is in danger of losing his job, he will change his mind — and then try to make it look as though he had been leading the way. The approach to Congress has to be through the arousal and organization of public opinion.

The question will remain "Is abortion *right?*" and it is a question that each of us must answer for himself. My beliefs and my experience have led me to conclude that the wisest public policy is to place the responsibility for that decision on the individual. The rightness or wrongness of an abortion depends on the individual case, and it seems to me clearly wrong to pass laws regulating all cases. But there is more to it than that. First, it is my view, and I think the majority's view, that abortion should always remain a last resort, never a primary method of limiting families. Contraceptive devices are the first choice: *devices,* because of their established safety compared to the controversial oral contraceptives. The weight of responsible medical opinion, by which I mean the opinions of qualified persons who have never been in the pay of the drug industry, seems to be that the question of the Pill's safety is not proven and that there are clear warnings that much more study is needed. So Pill research should continue, and meanwhile the emphasis — particularly in a publicly supported family planning program — should be on proven safe and effective methods. Beyond that, still from the standpoint of public policy, there must be far more stress on providing a full range of family planning services to persons of all economic levels. At present, the full gamut of services, from expert medical advice to, as a last resort, safe "legal" abortions, is available for the rich. Any woman who has the money and the sophistication about how things are done in our society can get an abortion within the law. If she is from a social stratum where such advice is available, she will be sent to a sympathetic psychiatrist and he will be well paid to believe her when she says she is ready to kill herself if she doesn't get rid of her pregnancy. But unless a woman has the $700 to $1000 minimum it takes to travel this route, her only safe course in most states is to have the child.

This means that, whether it was so intended, public policy as expressed in American abortion laws (excepting the handful of states where the repeal effort has succeeded) is to maximize illegitimacy. Illegitimate children have always been born and for the foreseeable future they will continue to be. Their handicap is not some legal blot on their ancestry; few intelligent persons give any thought to that today. The trouble is that illegitimate children are usually the most unwanted of the unwanted. Society has forced a woman to have a child in order to punish her. Our laws were based on the

Puritan reaction of "You've had your pleasure — now pay for it." But who pays? First, it is the helpless woman, who may be a girl in her early teens forced to assume the responsibility of an adult; young, confused, partially educated, she is likely to be condemned to society's trash heap as a result. But the child is often a worse loser. If his mother keeps him, she may marry or not (unmarried mothers are even less likely to marry than widows or divorcées). If she does not, she will have to neglect him and work at undesirable jobs to feed him, more often than not. His homelife will almost certainly be abnormal; he may survive it and even thrive, depending on his mother's personal qualities, but the odds have to be against him.

Of course, there should be no unwanted children. Whether they are legitimate or illegitimate is not of the first importance. But we will not even approach the ideal of having every child wanted, planned for, and cherished, until our methods of contraception are fully reliable and completely safe, and readily available to everyone. Until then, unwanted pregnancies will happen, in marriage and out of it. What is our public policy to be toward them? There are very few more important questions for society to face; this question is one that government has always avoided because it did not dare intrude on the sanctity of the home and marriage. But the catastrophic perils that follow in the train of overpopulation were not well known in the past and those perils were not imminent, so the question could be ducked. It cannot be any longer.

For all Americans, and especially for the poor, we must put an end to compulsory pregnancy. The well-off have only one problem when an unwanted pregnancy occurs; they must decide what they want to do and what they believe is right. For the poor, there is no such freedom. They started with too little knowledge about contraception, often with none except street lore and other misinformation. When trapped by pregnancy, they have only two choices, both bad — a cheap abortion or an unwanted child to plunge them deeper into poverty. Remember the statistics that show which choice is often taken: 49 percent of the deaths of pregnant black women and 65 percent of those of Puerto Rican women . . . due to criminal, amateur abortions.

Which is more like genocide, I have asked some of my black brothers — this, the way things are, or the conditions I am fighting for in which the full range of family planning services is freely available to women of all classes and colors, starting with effective contraception and extending to safe, legal termination of undesired pregnancies, at a price they can afford?

12

The Lindsay Campaign and Coalition Politics

THE 1969 MAYORALTY CAMPAIGN in New York City left me convinced that there are only two choices open for the Democratic party. Either it can reform itself and become truly "democratic," or it will watch its best elements split off and form the nucleus of a new party, together with some splinters from the Republican monolith and a large group of disaffected voters who belong to no party at present.

When John V. Lindsay failed to win renomination from his own Republican party, political experts agreed that he was finished. He was on the ballot as a Liberal nominee, but no one had ever won in New York City without the backing of one of the major parties. To a professional politician, whose faith is that nothing ever really changes even though issues come and go, the conclusion had to be that no one ever would win without major party backing. Lindsay did win, and the polls should have started to reexamine their axioms. It was their Belshazzar's feast. Even the message on the wall was the same one interpreted by Daniel: "God hath numbered thy kingdom and finished it; thou art weighed in the balances and art found wanting; thy kingdom is divided . . ."

What is happening in New York and other major cities is like what happened in my part of Brooklyn, starting twenty years earlier. The community has changed while the political bosses haven't. The white middle- and working-class voting blocs they have dealt with for years have trickled away. Those voters are in the suburbs now, where they are working as hard as they can to keep the housing barriers up against black and brown immigrants from the metropolis. The minorities have been confined to the city by a moat of bigotry. There, they are already the largest minority and they are steadily growing to a majority. In other big cities, such as Washington, Detroit, and Cleveland, the process is even further advanced. It is going to have profound effects on Democratic politics, which in the North has always rested on the powerful big city machines. Those machines are in the process of breaking down, and unless the Democratic party realizes it, it is going to become a minority group itself.

When Lindsay ran the first time on the Republican ticket in 1965, he won even though New York City has a large Democratic margin of registered voters. The reason was that he seemed more in tune with the social, economic, and racial problems of the city. People felt, somehow, that he might be able to help them. At least, he talked as though he understood, and they crossed party lines to follow him. The second time around, it looked different. His personally created patchwork coalition was in pieces. He had lost his support among the large and politically active group of white liberal Jewish voters, it appeared to the prophets, and this was going to cost him the mayoralty. One of the two "conservatives" the major parties had nominated was clearly going to win, and the odds were that it would be the Democrat, Mario A. Procaccino.

The situation was a king-sized headache for me, because I was not only a leader of the black community in one of the five boroughs, I was also a Democratic national committeeman. There are two from each state and I became one of New York's at the Chicago national convention in 1968, two months before I was elected to Congress. It was impossible for me to support Procaccino. His background, his statements, and his speeches gave black voters every reason to suspect that he was hostile to them. He seemed cut from the same cloth as the Republican nominee, a reactionary in the strict sense of the word. To the painful problems caused by social change, his solution was clearly to try to restore the way things used to be.

A Lindsay staff member called me soon after the primary and asked me whether I was going to support Procaccino.

"In good conscience, I cannot," I told him.

"What are you going to do?"

I didn't know myself. I told him I would have to think it over and make a decision in a few days. Most other black Democrats were straddling, and would continue to all through the campaign. They did not want to work for Procaccino and they didn't dare back Lindsay. Eventually the black and Spanish-speaking communities became generally disgusted with their political leaders for this mugwump behavior. What the voters did not realize was that black politicians are no different from white politicians. To all of them, the party is the main thing and the people come second, if that far up.

My closest advisers — Conrad, Mac Holder, and a few others — strongly urged me not to back Lindsay. They were frightened of the drastic consequences of my breaking with the party. I did not consult with any of the party higher-ups. There was just nowhere for me to go but over to Lindsay, unless I wanted to sit out the election. Too much was at stake. Lindsay was the only one of the three candidates who offered any hope that things would get better for the black community. I called the mayor and told him I would support him.

He arranged a press conference at Gracie Mansion and his press staff pulled out all the stops. It was the first encouraging thing that had happened in their campaign, some of Lindsay's campaign workers told me. They had been dispirited and felt the campaign was not moving. My endorsement gave them a ray of hope, a feeling that they just might win after all. They knew the political chance I was taking. They knew I was doing it out of conviction. No one had given me anything, no one had offered me anything, no one had pushed me. My only motive was that I thought Lindsay was the man who should be mayor of New York, given the choices available. The fact came through to the public, and I think it may have been a psychological turning point in the campaign. The phones at Gracie Mansion started ringing as soon as the announcement was made. Except for Senator Waldaba Stewart of Brooklyn, a member of the state legislature, no other black leader had endorsed Lindsay at that point. Wally appeared at Gracie Mansion with Lindsay and me that day to announce his backing. Percy Sutton spoke for the mayor later in the campaign, and Adam Powell joined the Lindsay camp the day before the election.

Naturally, the Procaccino camp was furious. I had touched them in their sore spot. Procaccino and Westchester County leader William Luddy demanded that I be kicked out as national committeeman. I reminded them publicly that no one asked President Roosevelt to resign his office when he supported Fiorello La Guardia, a Republican, for mayor in the 1930s. Some other black political leaders scolded me. I told them that no one has a right to call himself a leader unless he dares to lead. That means standing up to be counted on the side of his people, even at the risk of his political security. It means giving clear direction, so the people do not have to guess where you stand. Most of the black leaders in New York City ducked their responsibilities in the 1969 mayoral campaign. They hid their real feelings, or tried to make them known by dropping hints instead of committing themselves.

I made every effort my time allowed in Lindsay's behalf. I spoke with him at rallies, rode in motorcades, made radio and television spots, and had my picture with him on campaign posters that were plastered all over the city. Gradually other Democratic and Liberal leaders made their support for the mayor known. When Lindsay won, everybody claimed to have been on his side all along. I would never claim that my support made the difference. The campaign was so large and complex that no one can establish the weight of one element of the situation. That does not matter. What does matter is the significance of the victory. Lindsay was reelected because he appealed to a constituency that cuts across party lines. To the voters who had been turned off by regular two-party politics he offered a live alternative, and they combined to elect him.

Was it a unique case, or is it a portent of the future? I believe that it is a portent, and that it foretells an era of coalition politics and an eclipse of the traditional parties, at least in the larger cities. The day of issues and the man has arrived, and the time of labels and the party has passed. Citizens are going to demand that they have a voice in the political process from the start, and whenever five or six old-style political bosses meet clandestinely to pick a candidate, they are going to find themselves rejected at the polls.

Coalition politics is issue oriented instead of party oriented. It draws together disparate groups, who combine — temporarily, in all probability — around some issue of overriding importance to them at that time and place. By its nature, it confronts the traditional politics of expediency and compromise. It is called into being by the failure of compromises and the shabby results of action taken out of expediency. It is not a comfortable kind of political action for its leaders, because it involves creativity, innovation, change, and commitment to the people instead of to personal advancement. It means opening up participation to the out-groups as well as the in-groups, and giving real power instead of token representation to the minorities, at the policy-making and administrative levels. It means real effort to make the base as broad as possible and the leadership as responsive as possible to the needs of a wide and various constituency. This, of course, sounds like the ideal picture that the leaders of the existing political parties have of themselves. It is. But they have fallen so far from that ideal that they may be beyond redemption. I have not yet given up hope of redeeming the Democratic party. If I had, I wouldn't still be in it.

Our society is going through such turbulent changes that it is hard to picture how a new political movement can be given a lasting form. What is applicable now may be thrown out in a year or two. Values are constantly being reassessed. Until our dynamic and unhappy society struggles through to a new form of stability, until answers are found that again satisfy the majority, coalitions will keep forming and reforming. They will have to be loose, but they can be cohesive enough to succeed. They will include reformers of the familiar kind in New York City politics, independents of many stripes, some professionals, a large part of the "college voters," students, women's liberation groups, minority organizations, labor and liberal factions that are honestly progressive, and many other elements. Even if they do not form a majority at first, they will have an impact. In New York, they are making the old bosses of the Democratic party take notice. When the New Democratic Coalition held its own convention and agreed on its own slate of candidates for state offices in the 1970 campaign, the professional leaders were outraged. This fanatical bunch was putting them on the spot by meeting to make its choices in a democratic way, and making them look bad with their candidates selected in a back room. That traditional method of selecting candidates is the reason why Democrats, with great superiority in numbers, have been unable to elect a candidate to a major office in New York State for years. The bosses' hand-picked nominees are unacceptable to the voters, who retaliate in the only way they can by electing Republicans. Reform of the method of choosing candidates is the keystone of the new politics. Unless nominees are chosen democratically, with the widest possible participation in the process, nothing else really matters.

The first effective revolt in my time against boss rule in New York was at the 1964 gubernatorial nominating convention in Buffalo where I played a part in the uprising. After the convention had nominated Frank O'Connor according to the script, the bosses retired to the Statler Hilton to agree on a lieutenant governor nominee. I had made one of the seconding speeches for Howard J. Samuels, who lost badly, and I was the only Samuels supporter in the 186-member Kings County delegation. I had met him several years earlier at an educational conference and was impressed by the way he was

talking even then about changing our institutions so that they
worked for people. That kind of talk alienates politicians,
and he came to the convention a complete outsider. After
O'Connor won, Samuels and his family started packing their
bags to leave Buffalo. I stopped at his hotel room and found
him depressed, his wife bewildered, and some of the children
in tears. "Unpack," I said. "It's not over yet."

Back at the convention hall I found J. Raymond Jones,
the black Manhattan County leader. All the other big county
leaders were at the hotel — Joseph Crangle of Erie County,
Stanley Steingut of Brooklyn, William Luddy of Westchester,
and the others — deciding whom they were going to stuff
down the throats of their robot delegates.

"Ray," I asked him, "how come you're not over at the
Statler Hilton?"

"Those b———," he said. They had not thought him
worth inviting, assuming that whatever they decided would
have to be all right with him.

"You go down that side of the hall and I'll go down this
side, and let's see if we can get something happening," I told
him. I started with two upstate delegations, who had been
strong Samuels supporters and did not like what was going
on. Ray and I got delegate after delegate to pick up dis-
carded SAMUELS FOR GOVERNOR signs and write in "Lt." in
front of the word "Governor." Some of them got on chairs
and started to lead a chant, "We want Howie."

Jones went up to the podium, and as the bosses came back
from the hotel where they had agreed that Orrin Lehman
was going to be the nominee, they were astonished to hear
Jones shout, "New York County casts eighty-two votes for
Howard Samuels!" Soon everyone was shouting. It was beautiful. We had never dreamed it would work. One woman

from my Kings County delegation kissed me and said, "We wanted Howard, but we couldn't do anything."

"What do you mean, you couldn't do anything?" I asked her.

Samuels was nominated and ran with O'Connor. If Howard had led the ticket that year, I believe Nelson A. Rockefeller might not have been reelected. The delegates wanted Samuels, not the man they were coerced into choosing, and the voters would have felt the same way.

I went home from the convention with a blot on my copybook in the party leadership's eyes. But it was also dawning on them that I promised to become someone to reckon with in state politics. After the Lindsay election, that promise came true. Some of the consequences have been surprising. During the jockeying before the April 1970 nominating convention, I was approached by emissaries from most of the senatorial and gubernatorial hopefuls. One wanted to know how much Howard Samuels, my choice for the nomination, had paid me. He was ready to top it. When I told him Samuels had paid me nothing and that my support was not for sale, he didn't seem to believe me. Another of the go-betweens told me I was crazy. "You're the hottest thing on the New York political scene right now," he said. "Get your price."

"Chisholm," I have been advised, "you've got the brains, you've got the appeal to the voters, but you need more than that. You need money. You need an organization." The word *organization* is used a lot to frighten political newcomers. I have studied some of the organizations that people claim they have and discovered just how weak and ineffective they can be. Organizations are composed of people, and their strength is in proportion to the commitment of their members to the cause. A lot of political organizations are paper tigers, a big lie that old politicians use to scare away the competition.

I have an organization of my own, but it's not based on money or patronage or mutual aggrandizement. I can pick up a telephone and have 100 people at my house in an hour, ready to go to war. The reason is they know I am for them and will not sell them out for my own advantage. That's my personal kind of coalition politics. It will work for anyone who has enough sincerity and determination. If more people start by passing the traditional political parties that have failed them, those parties will either reform themselves or die. That's the goal: change the system. Shake it up, make it change in order for it to survive. It's not necessary to dump it, only to make it work.

13

Black Politicians and the Black Minority

BROTHERHOOD WEEK makes me sick. The original idea may have been fine, but it was naive. I have seen too many racists serve on Brotherhood Week committees, pretending to be decent human beings for seven days. What about all the other fifty-one weeks of the year? When people asked me to speak at Brotherhood Week events, I used to ask them, "What else are you doing? What are you doing about open housing? About schools? About fair employment and job training?" Now I don't get into that. I just say, "No thanks. Invite me to speak at some other event and I'll try to make it then." I'm not going to take part in a sterile ceremony by which hypocrites pretend to be cleansing themselves of the guilt of the racism they practice the rest of the time.

Much of the hypocrisy of Americans on the subject of race seems to be unconscious. Perhaps self-deception would be a better word for it. Racism is so universal in this country, so widespread and deep-seated, that it is invisible because it is so normal. Whites are furious when they are accused of it, as the Kerner report accused them when it exposed white racism as the cause of the urban riots of the 1960s. "Who,

us?" everyone from President Johnson down demanded in-
dignantly. They could not see the truth in front of their eyes.
It was not even a conclusion, but a visible fact. All they had
to do was look at the cities, surrounded by a fortified ring of
lily-white suburbs. Who built the suburbs and kept them
white? Who compelled poor black and Spanish-surnamed
citizens to crowd into the oldest, most run-down parts of the
cities? Who ran the school systems so that the slum schools
got the oldest textbooks, the greenest teachers, the least equip-
ment?

One experience that keeps recurring to me is a meeting I
had just before Christmas 1968 with a group of redcaps from
Penn Station. Not many people know that a majority of these
porters, elderly men now, have college degrees. When they
got out of school during the depression, they discovered that
what they had been told about education being the way out
of poverty was not true for black men. They have spent their
lives growing gnarled and bent carrying white travelers' bag-
gage for nickels and dimes. Imagine the waste — the human
potential that they once had, the loss to our society when they
were denied a chance to serve it as they were ready and able
to do. One told me with tears in his eyes, "Keep on fighting,
for all the black children." He was reconciled to the fact that
it was too late for him to have a fair chance, but he did not
want it to happen to another generation. Something happened to me as I talked to those men. I resolved that I'll die
if necessary to prevent their experience from being repeated
anymore.

On a speaking date in 1969 in St. Louis, a white member of
the audience asked me a question that I have heard repeatedly. It makes me more furious each time I hear it, until I
think it's a good thing I don't have a gun, or I would use it.
"What do you Negroes want now?" he asked me. "You all

aren't doing too bad. As a matter of fact, you're doing a lot better than some of the white people."

My God, what do we want? What does any human being want? Take away an accident of pigmentation of a thin layer of our outer skin and there is no difference between me and anyone else. All we want is for that trivial difference to make no difference. What can I say to a man who asks that? All I can do is try to explain to him why he asks the question.

"You have looked at us for years as different from you that you may never see us really. You don't understand because you think of us as second-class humans. We have been passive and accommodating through so many years of your insults and delays that you think the way things used to be is normal. When the good-natured, spiritual-singing boys and girls rise up against the white man and demand to be treated like he is, you are bewildered. All we want is what you want, no less and no more."

At one time a lot of us hoped that all it would take was to convince the white majority of the simple truth and justice of our cause, and the day of equality would dawn. That was the faith that created and sustained the civil rights movement of the 1950s and early 1960s. The movement was a failure. Everyone who was deeply involved in it hates to admit that. When one remembers the exhilaration that came from linking hands and singing, "Black and white together . . . We shall overcome," it is hard to believe that in spite of all the passion, the sacrifices, and the idealism that the civil rights movement called forth, it left little behind it but some new laws that have yet to be really enforced. The goal of the movement — integration — was not accomplished. It was not even brought closer, and that fact has at least temporarily discredited the goal.

Frustration at its failure split the civil rights movement

along racial lines. One fragment became the core of the white New Left; the other developed into the militant, activist, young black movement. Two different groups were equally outraged, the older, white activists and the black middle class. Both misunderstood and were horrified by the concept of Black Power. To their minds, Stokely Carmichael and George Wallace had the same goal — rigid segregation of the races. That interpretation of Black Power was a shortsighted one. Perhaps the young black leaders who hit upon the concept did not realize it, but they had grasped a real American political truth.

In schools they still teach about the melting pot, a turn-of-the-century idea that the United States has accepted all kinds of immigrants and turned them into Americans. Closer inspection reveals that the white minorities are not yet melted into the society, even after two or three generations. The care that politicians take to balance their tickets, figuring on the Irish Catholic vote, the Jewish vote, the Polish vote, and so on, proves the point. These groups are, obviously, more nearly assimilated than the stubborn, refractory black element of the population. But before they began to blend in, they had first to raise themselves to a level fairly equal to that of the rest, economically in particular. To do so, they had to advance not as individuals but as groups. They built political and economic power structures of their own within the larger society — stores, banks, businesses of all sorts, and a professional class of doctors, preachers, and teachers. Then they truly became enfranchised when they had power to wield. The history of the Kennedy family illustrates the evolution. So does that of many less famous Irish, Italian, and other immigrant-stock families. Barred at first from the opportunities that were open to the old elite, they made their way by serving their own communities and built their political power bases there. Successful blacks who are proud of their own accomplishments should not disregard the fact that despite their own efforts, they owe most of their success to the momentum of their group, to actions taken before they came of age.

How can the black minority, oppressed for more than 300 years, move forward to full citizenship? Not one by one, on the strength of individual talents and luck. That only works for a few. It means abandoning their identity, their birthrights. At the price of becoming pseudowhites, we have been admitted in small numbers as probationary members of American society. "Integration" on those terms was an idea that was foredoomed to be rejected by the mass of black Americans. What does it matter to them that their race has produced a few Ralph Bunches, Sammy Davises, and Percy Suttons? It does not close or even appreciably narrow the gulf between them and the greater society. That this gulf would be bridged by efforts from the white side was the dream of the civil rights movement. It was a beautiful dream, but it was mainly the creation of a small group of white idealists who did not understand their own society. They did not know the facts of life, that all Americans are the prisoners of racial prejudice. Even the civil rights crusaders were racists, in a subtle but no less destructive way. They ran the civil rights show, as they would later run the poverty show: "All right, here's what we're going to do." And their black allies believed and cooperated because they wanted so deeply to believe that it was the start of something new and wonderful, a gradual complete change of heart by the white majority. They were expecting a miracle, and of course no miracle happened.

When this became clear at last, the civil rights movement broke in two along the color line. It will never be joined again, because the fallacy on which it was founded has been demonstrated to blacks. They had thought that the custodians of power were going to be persuaded to surrender some of that power out of the simple goodness of their hearts. No way. Frederick Douglass had gone through the same evolution 100 years earlier and ended with the stark conclusion, "Power concedes nothing without a struggle."

What does it mean, in this context, to struggle? Does it mean individual violence or mass armed rebellion, burning, looting, shooting? There are, of course, young blacks and whites who have reached this point. Their last hope has vanished and they have resolved to bring the temple of their enemies down in ruins on the heads of everyone in it. It has not become clear to me yet that such tragic heroism is the only course of action left.

A number of myths cloud the vision of white Americans even when they make a sincere effort to see and understand their black fellow citizens. One of the most pernicious is the idea of the "ghetto." White sociologists applied this word, which had a precise meaning once in Europe, to black slum neighborhoods in this country and thereby did what intellectuals are noted for: they applied a label to a human problem and made it impossible to think about it.

What most whites think of when they say "ghetto" is a black slum. To them, all black communities are alike — run-down, crime-ridden jungles. When blacks use the word "ghetto" they almost always prefix it with "so-called," to reject this white stereotype. Of course, "ghetto" originally contained some insight; it is only because it has come to be a loaded word that I would discard it. Although black communities run the gamut from filthy slums to comfortable, stable residential sections, they *are* ghettos in the sense that their residents have to live there. The unwritten laws, the racist attitudes of the greater society, draw a circle around them and make it nearly impossible for them to break through.

A recent experience of my own may cast some light on the subject of ghettoization and illustrate that it is not poverty, lack of education, and lack of will that keeps black, brown, red, and yellow Americans behind the bars of segregation. I had always wanted to buy a house, but never felt able to do so until I was elected to Congress. Conrad and I had saved enough money, but the way the politicians kept redistricting Brooklyn, I never dared to settle down for fear my Assembly district would be changed and I would suddenly be living outside it. But the congressional district was so large I could not see how this could ever happen, so I started looking for a house. We found one we thought was perfect. When we tried to buy it, it was suddenly and inexplicably unavailable. A week later, the real estate agent found out that I was a member of Congress. Apparently this frightened him, and he called me back to tell me that the house was available after all. "Why didn't you tell me who you were?" he wailed. I told him off in the strongest language and we bought another house.

The sequel of the story, parenthetically, is that the New York State legislature redrew congressional district lines in 1970. The boundary of the new district that includes most of my present one, plus the Ocean Hill–Brownsville neighborhood which I had not represented, falls one block from my house. Temporarily, I live one block outside my congressional district. It is enough to make we wonder whether someone did not first find out exactly where I bought my house, and then drew the new district line.

The fact that I ran into racism when I tried to buy a house, even in Brooklyn, even after I had been elected to Congress, is significant. But if I had had no trouble that would have meant nothing, because my position could make me an exception. For the bars to be let down a little for me here and a little there has no relevance to most of my brothers and sisters. This brings us back to the point that for there to be real progress for us, we must all move ahead together, and we must do it ourselves.

Education, no doubt, is the key to long-range progress, although jobs and decent housing are the immediate needs. But the example of the Penn Station redcaps has to be kept in mind. Education alone will not be enough, even a college education. And it is obvious that not all blacks any more than all whites are college material, as we now define college. For the most part, the education provided for black children is a kind designed to keep them in their place. The story starts way back, during the time after the Civil War when at least three white groups were contending for control of the four million freed slaves. Abolitionists and other northern liberals wanted to educate the freedmen to "level all vestiges of the past," as Horace Mann Bond put it. If they had prevailed, American history would have been far different. But of course they could not prevail. Arrayed against them were southern conservatives and southern liberals, each with their own ideas, and they were strengthened by the uninterested, apathetic majority in the North.

The southern conservative knew education for blacks meant potential black economic and political power, which would make it impossible for them ever to restore the South as nearly as they could to the status quo ante bellum. They succeeded in discrediting Reconstruction with the libelous label of carpetbagging and attacked every agency that was working for progress with similar tactics — the Freedman's Bureau, for instance. Eventually they prevailed, with the help where needed of terrorist forces like the Klan, and re-established white supremacy with the infamous Black Codes, legitimized by the disgraceful Supreme Court "separate but equal" doctrine. Schools, medical care, the protection of the law — all were denied to black citizens as a matter of public policy in most of the South.

The reign of Jim Crow was a long and bloody one, and it is far from over yet, as the brutal killings of black students at Jackson State College reminded white America in the spring of 1970. But even when Jim Crow was at its height, there were southern whites who saw farther ahead than their neighbors, although they were equally unreconstructed. Their view, more subtle and dangerous, is still current, in the North as much as anywhere. Between the poles of complete repression and complete freedom for blacks and for any of our other racial minorities, there is another approach, that of using education as a means of continuing control over the lives of black people.

Many writers have pointed out, and I have used the analogy myself in speeches, that American blacks are in the position of a colonial population. They have been compelled to adopt the cultural standards and norms of their rulers in order to make any advancement whatever. But American blacks have been denied the option of a true colonized population; they have no true culture of their own to oppose to that of their exploiters, because theirs was systematically destroyed by the slave masters. They are uniquely vulnerable; it has been for them a choice of conform or die.

How can blacks be kept in a subordinate role forever? By using their vulnerability, the constraint they were under to conform to white values. It could best be done through the schools, to which blacks naturally flocked after the Civil War. They could be educated for service, and nothing else, and inculcated with attitudes of docility and industry. Many such schools were long ago established for blacks, if need be at private expense; if the schools were public, their programs were controlled to the same end.

Through the years I have heard black parents by the hundreds tell a modern, metropolitan version of the story: how their children, even if talented, were steered by teachers and counselors to a narrow range of jobs, to courses in vocational training, practical nursing, hairdressing, and so forth — never to academic courses that could lead to a professional or business career. Even now, there are very few black or Puerto Rican students graduated with academic diplomas from Brooklyn high schools.

Black leaders of the nineteenth century knew the need of their people for any kind of education. They knew the dangerous political and social context of their lives, so they took the poisoned half loaf and distributed it to their people. Perhaps they were right, at the time. They and their schools might not have survived at all if they had fought back and demanded equal treatment. It is the fashion now to malign George Washington Carver as the archetype of Uncle Tom. In Malcolm X's words, "The slavemaster took Tom and dressed him well, fed him well and even gave him a little education — a *little* education; gave him a long coat and a top hat and made all the other slaves look up to him. Then he used Tom to control them. The same strategy that was used in those days is used today."

It is necessary for our generation to repudiate Carver and all the lesser-known black leaders who cooperated with the white design to keep their people down. We need none of their kind today. Someday, when, God willing, the struggle is over and its bitterness has faded, those men and women may be rediscovered and given their just due for working, as best they could see to do in their time and place, for their brothers and sisters. But at present their influence is pernicious, and where they still control education, in the North or the South, they must be replaced with educators who are ready to demand full equality for the oppressed races and fight for it at any cost. The days of mind-deadening "industrial education" and of turning out half-trained black professionals to practice in the black community are not yet past, and it is time that they were. This chapter in the history of black America is another proof of the justice of black demands for control of their own institutions, particularly the schools. How can we trust even the most benevolent-appearing white, when we have seen through the years how a trap was concealed in nearly every "gift" we have been offered?

There is no longer any alternative for black Americans but to unite and fight together for their own advancement as a group. Everything else has been tried, and it has failed. This brings us again to the hardest question: How shall that fight be waged? Must it be with bullets, bombs, and guerrilla armies? God help me if I ever decide that there is no course left but that of destruction. I can feel in myself sometimes an anger that wants only to destroy everything in its path. There is a point at which passions as great as those that burn in the hearts of black Americans will not be frustrated any longer. If all the outlets are kept closed, they will at last burst out in a suicidal frenzy. I am not yet at that point. But everywhere, particularly in city neighborhoods like my district, there are thousands of young people who are almost ready to break loose, and there are militant groups urging them to do it. Unlike many black politicians, I still have an open line to them. The Panthers, the Moslems (black and orthodox), the Republic of New Africa, and other groups grow stronger and stronger. So far they do not consider me a sellout, as they do most black leaders. We talk. We have common ground. They try to show me where I'm wrong, and I try to show them where their thinking is negative and their plans self-defeating.

"I'm not a fool, brothers and sisters," I have told extremist groups. "I'm a pragmatist. What is the sense of shooting, burning, killing? What will it bring? All they have to do is press a button in Washington and every black neighborhood will be surrounded with troops and bayonets. What are you going to do against the massive forces of the government? You can't fight this kind of a struggle with matchsticks. You are fourteen or fifteen percent of the population, with no real economic or political power. When you get through burning, won't you still have to go to the Man and ask for an apartment?"

When I say this, they don't have an answer.

"Who do you see suffering?" I ask them. "Black women and children. Are you able to give them an alternative by leading them into battle? You have no program because you have no power. Your program is rhetoric, and rhetoric never won a revolution yet. Until we begin to use our brainpower to rattle this structure, they're only going to laugh. They'll still be sitting around their conference tables, and you're going to have to knock on the door and say, 'We need a grant . . .'"

They tell me, "Sister, you sound good, but we've got to fight."

"I am fighting," I tell them. "I know I'm here in Congress, part of the Establishment, but you can see that I haven't started to conform. I haven't sold out. I'm fighting within the system. There is no other place to fight, if you only understood it. There's no other way for us to survive, because we really don't have anything. I realize it's too slow for many of you. Maybe it's not much I'm doing yet, but it's a beginning. At least I can shake up powerful people. If you truly understood what power is, you would learn the weaknesses and the strengths of what you're fighting. You wouldn't go out there and say, 'I'm going after Whitey.' Going after Whitey's what? You can't change the system or anything else unless you know what you're about. You're just wasting energy."

I used to be a moderate. I spent twenty years going to all kinds of meetings, trying to find ways all of us, black and white, could work together. Thousands like me kept saying, "Let us in a little. Give us a piece of the pie." What happened? Watts, Newark, Hartford. And what was the reaction? We started to hear a new jargon about "the urban crisis" and "law and order" and "crime in the streets."

Today I am a militant. Basically I agree with what many of the extremist groups are saying — *except* that their tactics are wrong and too often they have no program. But people had better start to understand that if this country's basic racism is not quickly and completely abolished — or at least controlled — there will be real, full-scale revolution in the streets. I do not want to see that day come. But I think often of what Malcolm once said about freedom: "You get your freedom by letting your enemy know that you'll do anything to get your freedom. Then you'll get it. It's the only way you'll get it."

Black Americans today are serving that notice on white-oriented institutions. They are saying they are ready to do anything. In this, there is a great deal of talk about black nationalism. There is, in short, much talk. But after enough time, we will be tired of talking. When we look at the condition of black Americans in a historic context, we are forced to conclude that there has been relatively little change in our condition. Worse yet, we are forced to realize that there are relatively few means that we can use to change our position in the society. We are not the only ones, if you consider that roughly 2 percent of the people of this country control 80 percent of the resources and wealth. One has to be very good at make-believe to think that the remaining 98 percent are controlling anything. They are, in fact, being controlled by others. Just because all the hands on the reins of power are white, it does not follow that all whites have their hands on that power. But they feel that they do. This fact is important, because it reveals to us one of the major functions of racism in this society.

Racism keeps people who are being managed from finding out the truth through contact with each other. It serves the insidious purpose of the wars in George Orwell's novel *1984*. Orwell's imaginary world is a lot like the real world for black Americans today. But many of us, and most whites, have consistently refused to accept that they live in a managed society where conflict between the races is maintained and managed because it serves a purpose.

One of the functions of racism is to force black Americans to take the simplistic view that all whites are powerful, just because they are white. White Americans generally link up psychically with the statement, "We control." Blacks are supposed to connect psychically with the corollary, "Whites are in control, as we are powerless." Before we make any change in the way this country functions, which is to benefit a small ruling minority, whites and blacks will have to learn that the true statement should be "Some whites control this country and much of the world, for their own purposes."

How can we define a role in this society for the black politician? First, whether he represents an urban or a rural black district or a racially-split one, there is one thing he should never forget — that he is black. Because his opponents won't forget it, nor will the electorate. A case in point is the 1969 mayoral campaign in Los Angeles. Thomas Bradley, a black candidate, won the primary with 47 percent of the vote to 46 percent for the incumbent, Samuel Yorty. Since neither had a majority there had to be a run-off. Nearly everyone, except Yorty, thought Bradley would be an easy winner. Yorty was right. He beat Bradley — by running a white campaign. Bradley avoided the fact that he was black and Yorty made use of it. Yorty talked about law and order. Every black voter knew and every white voter should have known that he was talking about "rioting niggers." He charged Bradley with being antipolice and having a former Communist party worker as a key aide. Bradley had been a policeman in Los Angeles for twenty-one years. Yorty had been accused repeatedly of having the most graft-riddled administration in the country. Had both candidates been white, voters would have ignored the charges.

Bradley's mistake was in reacting as a white politician would, by keeping silent. He forgot that voters, white *and* black, will believe things about a black candidate that they will not readily believe about a white one. The black leader has less leeway; he must conform to higher standards, or he will be shot down by some one of the enemies who are after him. Adam Clayton Powell, for instance, was punished by Congress for behavior that would not have disturbed most of his colleagues if he had been white. For other committee chairmen who have, as is common knowledge in Washington, done far more censurable things, the system has found ways of making accommodations. Tom Bradley should have heeded the lesson: you get no breaks if you are black. Had he been white, Yorty's clumsy attacks would have rolled off his back and Bradley would be mayor of Los Angeles. I think he would have won, if he had not forgotten that he is black and therefore more vulnerable.

This raises the question of whether black politicians can be elected where the electorate is not solidly black. I believe the answer is yes, sometimes. But to do so they must stay aware of six points Georgia State legislator Julian Bond outlined in the second issue of *The Black Politician:*

1. Social, economic, education, political and physical segregation and discrimination fill a very real need for the white majority.
2. Appeals to justice and fair play are outmoded and useless when power, financial gain and prestige are at stake.
3. Positions of segregation and discrimination will be adhered to until change is forced through coercion, threats, power or violence.
4. Initiative for black political organization and education must come from within the Negro community and must be sustained on a day-to-day basis.
5. The geographical distribution of Negroes makes Negro-white coalitions desirable, but only when based on racial self-interest and genuine equality between the coalescing groups.
6. Racial self-interest, race consciousness and racial solidarity must always be paramount in the words and deeds of blacks in politics; when self-interest is forgotten, organized racism will continue to dominate and frustrate the best-organized actions of any black political unit, and leave it powerless and defenseless.

Another way of putting it is that for our freedom struggle to advance in the political arena, black politicians have to accept their blackness. They have to form an ideological base from which to operate, and that base has to be founded on their color. In doing this, they may even start a new political movement. Julian foresaw the possibility in the same article and said this new movement "must address itself to solving America's white problem, to developing a new consciousness in the black and white communities."

Charles Evers, the black mayor of Fayette, Mississippi, ran the kind of campaign that Julian is calling for. His summation of it makes the point quite clear. "We ran a hard, clean race, we talked about nothing but the issues," Evers told an interviewer. "I didn't even bring the white folks up, because I didn't want to give them any credit at all. I never discuss them. All I discussed was what we gotta have and what we are gonna do and how we are going to change the system, and what we are going to do for the poor people. I mostly ran a poor people's campaign. And I think the white votes I got were poor whites. Because they know they are subjected to the same type of things that Negroes are — maybe on a different basis, but it is still the same denial and discrimination."

What Evers implies is that disenfranchised people throughout the country must begin to disregard party and racial labels. That is, I believe, extremely important. It will do black Americans absolutely no good to be politically and economically enfranchised into a system that systematically denies human values and destroys the environment that sustains life. By affirming and fighting for the values that are life sustaining, black politicians can become the vanguard of the forces that will save this country, if it is to be saved.

It is estimated that there are now about 1500 black elected officials in the United States, about 600 of them in the South. At present, the ten black members of Congress must be considered significant mainly for their symbolic value. They are so few that, even were they more unified into a bloc than they are, their effect would be negligible — except for that which they exert as individuals. But blacks are running for and winning office at every level. There are now more than 450 school board members, more than 450 city councilmen and other local officials, and some 200 state officials, chiefly legislators. There are 55 mayors, 100 county officials, and 175 judges, marshals, and sheriffs.

We have no adequate profile of the average black elected official yet, but it is apparent that they are overwhelmingly male — a trend that I have to deplore, because the most disenfranchised and exploited minority in this country is still its women. More women must come to the forefront, but I do not think that they have to do so at the expense of black male candidates. There are too many offices held by the declared enemies of both groups for blacks and women to fight over who is going to run. We should be concerned with finding and running every qualified candidate we can for every office that is open, from county commissioner to U.S. senator and for President and Vice President.

The majority of black elected officials are registered either as Democrats or Independents. Only about fifty to fifty-five, it is estimated, are Republicans. But under whatever label, most of them seem to share a distaste for following the old party lines. The average age of black elected officials is somewhat lower than that of white ones, and that may be because the growing tone of militancy in the black community demands youth. There are still old-line black politicians around whose primary interest is lining their pockets, but it seems that the political atmosphere is growing more hostile to them and more friendly to candidates who are ready to question priorities, fight for what they believe, and refuse to compromise when they believe that a compromise is not good enough for those whom they represent. If it is true that the black electorate is becoming more sophisticated and more militant about positive change, as I am sure it is, the effect will be to demand that candidates be the best choice available to the community at the time. And even where the black element is not dominant enough to elect black candidates, it can combine with other progressive forces to push younger, more socially committed white politicians into the arena. This could have a profound effect on the American political system.

Of course, all this theoretical discussion should not lead anyone to lose sight of the three basic elements of political action — registration, financing, and campaigning. Without these three foundations, successful political activity is impossible no matter how sophisticated its theoretical basis. People often ask me how I burst on the national political scene so quickly. What they fail to realize is that in Brooklyn there have been black people working toward political freedom for more than twenty years. They do not know the efforts of groups like the Bedford-Stuyvesant Political League, the Unity Democratic Club, and others that in all the Bedford-Stuyvesants of this country have been working, organizing, collecting, and fighting toward freedom from white political control of black communities.

From the beginning I felt that there were only two ways to create change for black people in this country — either politically or by open armed revolution. Malcolm defined it succinctly — the ballot or the bullet. Since I believe that human life is uniquely valuable and important, for me the choice had to be the creative use of the ballot. I still believe I was right. I hope America never succeeds in changing my mind.

Part IV
Looking Ahead

14

A Government That Cannot Hear the People

"F**OR THE FIRST TIME** in the history of the human race, a great nation is able and willing to make a commitment to eradicate poverty among its people. It will be a great program and it will succeed."

That was President Lyndon B. Johnson's boast as he signed the Economic Opportunity Act of 1964. The war on poverty began with tremendous fanfare and was waged with enormous outlays of money and effort. Thousands of dedicated persons spent all their talents on it. Why did it fail to close the gap between poverty and affluence in the United States? Was it the Vietnam war that stole away the tax money that should have gone into social programs?

Like the crusaders for civil rights, some poverty warriors still do not want to admit that their great venture was a flop. They prefer to blame Johnson's war, Congress, the city hall and courthouse, political crowds, and now the Nixon administration. There is justice in each of those indictments, but the main reason the war on poverty was lost was a failing that was built into it. The antipoverty programs were designed by white middle-class intellectuals who had no experience of being poor, despised, and discriminated against. They looked at the condition of the poor and made their diagnosis: lack of opportunity. All the other problems of the have-nots in our society — hunger, ignorance, crime, disease — were seen to be caused by the fact that when poor people tried to reach out for socially acceptable goals, they found their aspirations blocked.

So far, so good; this is true. But why is the way upward blocked? The poverty warriors described the cycle of deprivation: hunger, lack of education, lack of social mobility, leading to unemployability or low income potential, leading to frustration and poor motivation, leading in turn to hunger, poor education, and so on for the next generation. Break the cycle at one point and you end its vicious repetition. That was true, too, of course. Where do you start, with schools, health, housing, jobs, or what? Better employment was clearly the key, the planners decided. We will train the poor who are rejected and unhirable, and find them better jobs as they are able to handle them. The only fact left out of the analysis was the fundamental problem: racism.

Most of the poor were poor because they were labeled niggers or greasers or hillbillies or canucks or spics. They belonged to despised, powerless groups. There was no way the antipoverty strategists could see the importance of this factor. They knew about it theoretically, but they had not been there themselves. They didn't know where it was at. If they had gotten together with their "clients" in the poor communities from the start, things might have been different. Such involvement did come later, dictated by the growing understanding of program field workers.

The federal programs were intended to give the poor something tangible, quickly, and without alarming the middle class. Congress, in particular, did not want to cause any disruption of the political structure. The goal was to eliminate poverty without making any other major changes. Slowly the suspicion grew that the poor knew more about what they needed and how to get it than anyone else, if they were given a chance to get in on planning the programs. But this meant organization, and dealing with issues affecting jobs, schools, and housing meant that the organization of the poor soon got to be political. No top policy-makers wanted community action programs to become ways of achieving political power for the poor. Certainly few of the congressmen who voted for the establishment of the Office of Economic Opportunity would have done so if they had foreseen the Pandora's box that could be opened by organizing the poor. It was to have been a self-help program without the self.

Local politicians were quick to see the danger to them, and to demand that "maximum feasible participation" of the poor be played down in the design of the antipoverty programs. If people started to get together to help themselves, with the resources of the federal government to help them, who would need the ward politicians, the district leaders, the clubhouse lawyers, the courthouse gang? So the local politicians' response was to take charge wherever they could, and usually they could; they made sure the representatives of the poor were hand-picked, middle-class, and "responsible" leaders who had more in common with the existing power structures than with the truly deprived. It did not take long for the mass of the poor to catch on that they were being defrauded once again. After that happens, it is unlikely that real participation in a program can be readily secured, or that it will be orderly and cooperative in nature.

But the antipoverty program is leaving behind it a legacy that was quite unexpected. It politicized blacks and other poor minority groups to a surprising degree, considering that the original programs had so little emphasis on organization, and that where effective organizations appeared they were not generally encouraged by those in power. Black Americans, in particular, partly because of the failures of OEO, began to understand that they had struggled too hard to fight prejudice and make it possible for individuals to win freedom and power, and not hard enough to build organizations on ethnic lines to achieve group power and freedom. Many kinds of economic self-help organizations have started to appear. It has also become increasingly clear to minorities that they cannot ignore the political arena. If they are going to enter the economic mainstream, they will have to become significantly involved in politics.

There is a clear lack of joy in political circles over this trend, which is evidence to me of its importance. Similarly, the fact that the present administration is dismembering OEO and turning its more successful programs over to older, more change-resistant bureaus and agencies tells me that OEO was, in spite of everything, achieving enough success in limited areas to make it worrisome to some people.

The history of the war on poverty shows, among other things, that people are learning to rebel against government that imposes on them policies that they had no hand in forming. The trend is visible in other areas of public life, particularly in education. But nowhere has the conflict between official policy and what the public wants been more bitter and prolonged than it has over the Southeast Asian war and its relation to domestic priorities. I had made my maiden speech against the war after I was forced to realize that the new President was not, despite what he said, acting to bring the war to a quick end. He was also moving to continue the development of fantastic weapons for future wars, at staggering costs, and to do so was quite willing to cut the heart out of social program after program — education, job training, housing, urban redevelopment.

Head Start, one of OEO's most successful programs and one especially significant to me as a specialist in early childhood education, was reduced. The Job Corps, just hitting its stride, was slashed in half. Real job training programs that prepared unskilled persons for worthwhile work were put on the shelf in favor of phony ones, which amounted to subsidizing businessmen so they could hire poor people at low cost to themselves. Those hired were kept in routine jobs for the period of "training" and then laid off when the subsidies ran out. The list was all but endless.

What was happening? How could a President be so unconcerned about the needs of the nation he headed, so unresponsive to the will of its citizens? What barrier kept the voices of the people from reaching him? Before the end of his first year in office, there came the Haynesworth nomination to the Supreme Court. When it was defeated, the Carswell nomination followed. I was aghast at this appeal to a sectional minority. When Carswell's 1948 white supremacist speech came to light, reporters called the black members of Congress for their reactions. I was so angry I instructed my staff not to put them through to me but to tell them: "Mrs. Chisholm has no comment. She says she can't be bothered to make a statement every time Nixon appoints a racist to the Supreme Court."

Then the administration tried to tear the heart out of the Voting Rights Act, the federal law that had made it possible, for more black citizens to register and vote in the deep South than ever before. Its cunning scheme was to ostensibly extend the law to the entire country, at the cost of removing the features that had made it work. It was pushed through the House by a coalition of Republicans and southern Democrats.

If it had become law it would have left action to protect voting rights in any locality up to the attorney general — the same attorney general who was at that moment paying the administration's campaign debts to the South by wrecking the progress of school desegregation through indefinite delay of legal action against southern school districts.

Southern schools, which had been given fifteen years of grace in complying with the law and the Constitution, began to get further delays. The White House, in mid-1969, issued a "new policy" on desegregation guidelines. It was so vague that no one could make out what it said except perhaps one district judge in Louisiana. Judge Ben C. Dawkins ordered HEW to renegotiate the school desegregation plans of thirty-seven Louisiana districts, of which the judge had earlier approved. Now he was calling the same plans "outrageous" and declaring that the new policy statement "gives us considerably more elbow room."

For more than a year the Nixon administration appeared to be wavering on school desegregation, but actually kept moving, behind a curtain of misdirection, straight toward a policy that would win the President every unreconstructed heart in Dixie. Finally he went all the way with his March 1970 statement on policy, appointing himself the guardian of the "neighborhood school," a code phrase that no segregationist could fail to catch and admire. He proclaimed that the federal government would not require busing beyond "normal geographic zones" and made it clear that Washington would have nothing whatsoever to say about de facto segregation.

The difference between de jure and de facto segregation is the difference between open, forthright bigotry and the shamefaced kind that works through unwritten agreements between real estate dealers, school officials, and local politicians. What the President said was that, as long as a locality can manage to keep its black, brown, and poor citizens jammed into filthy slums by conspiracy, rather than by statute, it is fine with him and no one in Washington will lose any sleep.

As an outrageous attack on school buses at Lamar, South Carolina, showed immediately thereafter, the Nixon southern strategy was playing with fire, because it encouraged the lowest, most racist elements in the South to believe that their day was not past after all. The result was a tragic setback for all the white and black southerners whose main desire is to progress together in peace and growing understanding. They had been making a beginning at that essential and difficult job. Gains had been made, but President Nixon helped to see that they were undone. It amazed me to hear a President refer, as he did in that statement, to "the notion" that all-black schools are inherently inferior. That "notion" has been the law of the land since the Supreme Court declared it to be in its 1954 decision on *Brown* v. *Board of Education,* and the President, by his oath of office, swore to uphold the Constitution.

His school desegregation policies and his Supreme Court appointments made it clear that Nixon does not want to be President of black, brown, and other dark-skinned Americans. His Vietnam policy turned out to be to keep the war going as long as possible, except with Vietnamese troops taking over in the combat areas. This meant that the estrangement of American youth from their own government would continue and grow more serious. And his decision to fight inflation by every means but the one effective one — ending the war — meant that there would be no real efforts made to attack housing, employment, nutrition, and education problems under his administration, because there would be no money in the budget to do it with.

Of all his errors, I believe that President Nixon's cynical, callous attitude toward his poor, black, brown, white, or red fellow citizens will turn out to be the most serious. It will be his undoing. His southern strategy will be his Vietnam. As President Johnson assured his own downfall by edging, step by step, into that disastrous and unpopular war, Nixon is trying to lead this country, step by step, in a direction that eventually, I pray, it will refuse to take.

But will it? My deep misgivings at the answer are not based on mere political opposition to President Nixon, nor even opposition to his Vietnam war policy or his school desegregation and voters' rights policies. The first two years of his administration made him a symbol to me, and I think to nearly every black American. He represents nearly every one of the deep-seated and tragic flaws of this society, as they appear to us. He does not care for his black fellow citizens; he does not even see them until he is forced to, and then deals with them grudgingly. He is able to disregard the misery of poor Americans of every color in order to squander our resources on a foreign military adventure in which this nation has no vital interest. We look to the 1972 election with anxiety. Will part of this nation rejoice at seeing the rest oppressed, and reward a leader who has cunningly manipulated its fears and prejudices? Or will a majority of voters insist on a leader — who he could be I cannot yet guess — who will appeal to their birthright of idealism and their love of justice, instead of to their heritage of racism and special privilege?

15

Women and Their Liberation

WHEN A YOUNG WOMAN graduates from college and starts looking for a job, one question every interviewer is sure to ask her is "Can you type?" There is an entire system of prejudice unspoken behind that question, which is rarely if ever asked of a male applicant. One of my top assistants in my Washington office has always refused to learn to type, although not knowing how has been an inconvenience, because she refused to let herself be forced into a dead-end clerical job.

Why are women herded into jobs as secretaries, librarians, and teachers and discouraged from being managers, lawyers, doctors, and members of Congress? Because it is assumed that they are different from men. Today's new militant campaigners for women's rights have made the point that for a long time society discriminated against blacks on the same basis: they were different and inferior. The cheerful old darky on the plantation and the happy little homemaker are equally stereotypes drawn by prejudice. White America is beginning to be able to admit that it carries racial prejudice in its heart, and that understanding marks the beginning of the end of racism. But prejudice against women is still acceptable because it is invisible. Few men can be persuaded to believe that it exists. Many women, even, are the same way. There is very little understanding yet of the immorality involved in double pay scales and the classification of the better jobs "for men only." More than half the population of the United States is female, but women occupy only 2 percent of the managerial positions. They have not yet even reached the level of tokenism. No woman has ever sat on the Supreme Court, or the AFL-CIO council. There have been only two women who have held cabinet rank, and at present there are none. Only two women now hold ambassadorial rank in the diplomatic corps. In Congress, there are one woman senator and ten representatives. Considering that there are about 3.5 million more women in the United States than men, this is outrageous.

It is true that women have seldom been aggressive in demanding their rights and so have cooperated in their own enslavement. This was true of the black population for many years. They submitted to oppression, and even condoned it. But women are becoming aware, as blacks did, that they can have equal treatment if they will fight for it, and they are starting to organize. To do it, they have to dare the sanctions that society imposes on anyone who breaks with its traditions. This is hard, and especially hard for women, who are taught not to rebel from infancy, from the time they are first wrapped in pink blankets, the color of their caste. Another disability is that women have been programmed to be dependent on men. They seldom have economic freedom enough to let them be free in more significant ways, at least until they become widows and most of their lives are behind them.

That there are no female Supreme Court justices is important, but not as important as the fact that ordinary working women by the millions are subjected to the most naked and unjustified discrimination, by being confined to the duller and less well-paid jobs or by being paid less than men for doing the same work. Here are a recent year's figures from the Labor Department: white males earned an average of $7179 a year, black males $4508, white women $4142, and black women $2934. Measured in uncontestable dollars and cents, which is worse — race prejudice or antifeminism? White women are at an economic disadvantage even compared to black men, and black women are nowhere on the earnings scale.

Guidance counselors discriminate against girls just as they have long done with young black or Puerto Rican male students. They advise a black boy to prepare for a service-oriented occupation, not a profession. They steer a girl toward her "natural career," of being a wife and mother, and plan an occupational goal for her that will not interfere too much with that aim. The girl responds just as the average young black does, with mute agreement. Even if she feels vaguely rebellious at the limitations being put on her future before it has even begun, she knows how the cards are stacked against her and she gives in.

Young minority-group people do not get this treatment quite as much as they did, because they have been radicalized and the country has become more sensitive to its racist attitudes and the damage they do. Women too must rebel. They should start in school, by rejecting the traditional education society considers suitable to them, and which amounts to educational, social, and economic slavery.

There are relevant laws on the books, just as there are civil rights laws on the books. In the 91st Congress, I am a sponsor of the perennial Equal Rights Amendment, which has been before every Congress for the last forty years but has never passed the House. It would outlaw any discrimination on the basis of sex. Men and women would be completely equal before the law. But laws will not solve deep-seated problems overnight. Their use is to provide shelter for those who are most abused, and to begin an evolutionary process by compelling the insensitive majority to reexamine its unconscious attitudes.

The law cannot do the major part of the job of winning equality for women. Women must do it themselves. They must become revolutionaries. Against them is arrayed the weight of centuries of tradition, from St. Paul's "Let women learn in silence" down to the American adage, "A woman's place is in the home." Women have been persuaded of their own inferiority; too many of them believe the male fiction that they are emotional, illogical, unstable, inept with mechanical things, and lack leadership ability.

The best defense against this slander is the same one blacks have found. While they were ashamed of their color, it was an albatross hanging around their necks. They freed themselves from that dead weight by picking up their blackness and holding it out proudly for all the world to see. They found their own beauty and turned their former shame into their badge of honor. Women should perceive that the negative attitudes they hold toward their own femaleness are the creation of an antifeminist society, just as the black shame at being black was the product of racism. Women should start to replace their negative ideas of their femininity with positive ones affirming their nature more and more strongly.

It is not female egotism to say that the future of mankind may very well be ours to determine. It is a fact. The warmth, gentleness, and compassion that are part of the female stereotype are positive human values, values that are becoming more and more important as the values of our world begin to shatter and fall from our grasp. The strength of Christ, Gandhi, and Martin Luther King was a strength of gentleness, understanding, and compassion, with no element of violence in it. It was, in short, a *female* strength, and that is the kind that often marks the highest type of man.

If we reject our restricted roles, we do not have to reject these values of femaleness. They are enduring values, and we must develop the capacity to hold them and to dispense them to those around us. We must become revolutionaries in the style of Gandhi and King. Then, working toward our own freedom, we can help the others work free from the traps of their stereotypes. In the end, antiblack, antifemale, and all forms of discrimination are equivalent to the same thing — antihumanism. The values of life must be maintained against the enemies in every guise. We can do it by confronting people with their own humanity and their own inhumanity whenever we meet them, in the streets, in school, in church, in bars, in the halls of legislatures. We must reject not only the stereotypes that others have of us but also those we have of ourselves and others.

In particular, I am certain that more and more American women must become involved in politics. It could be the salvation of our nation. If there were more women in politics, it would be possible to start cleaning it up. Women I have known in government have seemed to me to be much more apt to act for the sake of a principle or moral purpose. They are not as likely as men to engage in deals, manipulations, and sharp tactics. A larger proportion of women in Congress and every other legislative body would serve as a reminder that the real purpose of politicians is to work for the people.

The woman who gets into politics will find that the men who are already there will treat her as the high school counselor treats girls. They see her as someone who is obviously just playing at politics part-time, because, after all, her real place is at home being a wife and mother. I suggested a bright young woman as a candidate in New York City a while ago; she had unlimited potential and with good management and some breaks could become an important person to the city. A political leader rejected her. "Why invest all the time and effort to build up the gal into a household name," he asked me, "when she's pretty sure to drop out of the game to have a couple of kids at just about the time we're ready to run her for mayor?"

Many women have given their lives to political organizations, laboring anonymously in the background while men of far less ability managed and mismanaged the public trust. These women hung back because they knew the men would not give them a chance. They knew their place and stayed in it. The amount of talent that has been lost to our country that way is appalling. I think one of my major uses is as an example to the women of our country, to show them that if a woman has ability, stamina, organizational skill, and a knowledge of the issues she can win public office. And if I can do it, how much more hope should that give to white women, who have only one handicap?

One distressing thing is the way men react to women who assert their equality: their ultimate weapon is to call them unfeminine. They think she is antimale; they even whisper that she's probably a lesbian, a tactic some of the Women's Liberation Front have encountered. I am not antimale any more than I am antiwhite, and I am not antiwhite, because I understand that white people, like black ones, are victims of a racist society. They are products of their time and place. It's the same with men. This society is as antiwoman as it is antiblack. It has forced males to adopt discriminatory attitudes toward females. Getting rid of them will be very hard for most men — too hard, for many of them.

Women are challenged now as never before. Their numbers in public office, in the professions, and in other key fields are declining, not increasing. The decline has been gradual and steady for the last twenty years. It will be difficult to reverse at first. The women who undertake to do it will be stigmatized as "odd" and "unfeminine" and must be prepared to endure such punishment. Eventually the point will be made that women are not different from men in their intelligence and ability and that women who aspire to important jobs — president of the company, member of Congress, and so on — are *not* odd and unfeminine. They aspire for the same reasons as any man — they think they can do the job and they want to try.

For years to come, most men will jeer at the women's liberation groups that are springing up. But they will someday realize that countless women, including their own wives and especially their daughters, silently applaud the liberation groups and share their goals, even if they are unable to bring themselves to rebel openly. American women are beginning to respond to our oppression. While most of us are not yet revolutionaries, the time is coming when we will be. The world must be taught that, to use the words of Women's Liberation activist Robin Morgan, "Women are not inherently passive or peaceful. We're not inherently anything but human. And like every other oppressed people rising up today, we're out for our freedom by any means necessary."

16

Youth and America's Future

ONE QUESTION bothers me a lot: Who's listening to me? Some of the time, I feel dishearteningly small and futile. It's as if I'm facing a seamless brick wall, as if most people are deaf to what I try to say. It seems so clear to me what's wrong with the whole system. Why isn't it clear to most others? The majority of Americans do not want to hear the truth about how their country is ruled and for whom. They do not want to know why their children are rejecting them. They do not dare to have to rethink their whole lives. There is a vacuum of leadership, created partly by the bullets of deranged assassins. But whatever made it, all we see now is the same tired old men who keep trucking down front to give us the same old songs and dances.

There are no new leaders coming along. Where are they? What has happened suddenly? On the national level, on the state level, who commands respect, who is believed by a wide enough cross section of the population to qualify as a leader? I don't see myself as becoming that kind of a leader. My role, I think, is more that of a catalyst. By verbalizing what is wrong, by trying to strip off the masks that make people comfortable in the midst of chaos, perhaps I can help get things moving.

It may be that no one can have any effect on most adults in this society. It may be that the only hope is with the younger generation. If I can relate to them, give them some kind of focus, make them believe that this country can still become the America that it should have been, I could be content. The young may be slandered as "kooks" and "societal misfits" by frightened, demagogic old men, but that will not scare them. They are going to force change. For a while they may be beaten down, but time is on their side, and the spirit of this generation will not be killed. That's why I prefer to go around to campuses and talk with the kids rather than attend political meetings. Politicians tell me I'm wasting my time and energy. "They don't vote," I'm told. Well, I'm not looking for votes. If I were, I would get the same kind of reception that a lot of political figures get when they encounter younger people, and I would deserve it.

There are many things I don't agree with some young zealots about. The main one, I suppose, is that I have not given up — and will not give up until I am compelled to — my belief that the basic design of this country is right. What is essential is to make it work, not to sweep it away and substitute — what? Something far worse, perhaps.

Most young people are not yet revolutionary, but politicians and police and other persons in power almost seem to be conspiring to turn them into revolutionaries. Like me, I think, most of them are no more revolutionary than the founders of this country. Their goals are the same — to insure individual liberty and equality of opportunity, and forever to thwart the tyrannous tendencies of government, which inevitably arise from the arrogance and isolation of men who are securely in power. All they want, if it were not too unfashionable for them to say so, is for the American dream to come true, at least in its less materialistic aspects. They want to heal the gaping breach between this country's promises and its performance, a breach that goes back to its founding on a Constitution that denied that black persons and women were full citizens. "Liberty and justice for all" were beautiful words, but the ugly fact was that liberty and justice were only for white males. How incredible that it is nearly 200 years since then, and we have still to fight the same old enemies! How is it possible for a man to repeat the pledge of allegiance that contains these words, and then call his fellow citizens "societal misfits" when they are simply asking for liberty and justice?

Such schizophrenia goes far back. "All forms of commerce between master and slave are tyranny," intoned Thomas Jefferson, who is rumored to have had several children by black women on his estate. If the story is true, the great democrat was a great hypocrite. Even if it is not true, it has verisimilitude. It could be a perfect metaphor for the way our country was founded and grew, with lofty and pure words on its lips and the basest bigotry hidden in its heart.

The main thing I have in common with the kids is that we are tired of being lied to. What we want is for people to mean what they say. I think they recognize at least that I'm for real. They know most adults are selling something they can't deliver.

Nowhere nearly enough young persons are involved in politics. Too many have been discouraged from participating, for various reasons. Some retired into inactivity after 1968, the year when Robert Kennedy and Martin Luther King were killed, Eugene McCarthy was ignored by the men who controlled the Democratic convention, the Chicago police attacked them in the streets, and finally, Richard Nixon was elected President. It was a discouraging year for youth, a year when their hopes were trampled into the mud one after another. Not much since then has given young people any hint that the forces of reaction are not firmly in control.

One reason for youthful distaste for politics has been the fact that the eighteen to twenty-one-year-old population was for years our largest disenfranchised group. At eighteen, young persons were legally adults in most states, and could be prosecuted as grownups; they were enjoined to bear arms if called, and die if unlucky. They could see clearly that they were being given all of the duties and none of the privileges of citizenship. Congress has moved to correct this long-standing injustice; it remains to be seen how quickly and in how great numbers young people avail themselves of the ballot. It is my belief that in two or three years at most from the time Congress acted in the spring of 1970 the under-twenty-one voting bloc will be a major factor in political calculations, and a major force for progress.

The most tragic error into which older people can fall is one that is common among educators and politicians. It is to use youth as scapegoats for the sins of their elders. Is the nation wasting its young men and its honor in an unjust war? Never mind — direct your frustration at the long-haired young people who are shouting in the streets that the war must end. Curse them as hippies and immoral, dirty fanatics; after all, we older Americans could not have been wrong about anything important, because our hearts are all in the right place and God is always on our side, so anyone who opposes us must be insane, and probably in the pay of the godless Communists.

Youth is in the process of being classed with the dark-skinned minorities as the object of popular scorn and hatred. It is as if the United States has to have a "nigger," a target for its hidden frustrations and guilt. Without someone to blame, like the Communists abroad and the young and black at home, middle America would be forced to consider whether all the problems of our time were in any way its own fault. That is the one thing it could never stand to do. Hence, it finds scapegoats.

Few adults, I am afraid, will ever break free of the crippling attitudes that have been programmed into their personalities — racism, self-righteousness, lack of concern for the losers of the world, and an excessive regard for property. One reason, as I have noted, is that they do not know they are like this, and that they proclaim ideals that are the reverse of many of their actions. Such hypocrisy, even if it is unconscious, is the real barrier between them and their children. Individually and collectively, Americans can no longer get away with proclaiming their democratic faith and jealously guarding their special privileges. We cannot hope any longer to be believed when we claim to be defending freedom, after so many years of being seen to care nothing about the freedom of citizens of Latin American, Asian, European, and Caribbean nations where we prop up dictatorial regimes. The rest of the world sees through the sham, when we pour billions in "foreign aid," which is really military assistance, into underdeveloped countries where the citizens continue to starve — as do millions of our own.

If it is not too late for America to be saved, the young will save it — and the blacks, the Indians, the Spanish-surnamed, the young women, and the other victims of American society. They, if any, will become the conscience that the country has lacked. They will try to force it to practice what it has preached. Such sentiments have become such a cliché of oratory that I am afraid they have lost all force. They must be taken seriously. I have traveled, I have spoken to, I have looked at too many young persons, black and white, not to take these ideas seriously. I have looked in their faces and seen something I had never seen before, even in the faces of white students, suburban children in their early teens. They are ready to die for their convictions. Their parents do not know what they think. They could never believe that their children have reached such a point. But these young people — so young, so strangely attractive — have resolved that the United States must become the society it has always claimed to be, and that they will make it so. If those in power will not respond to their simple demands for justice, their violent young hands will be laid upon the structure of the social and political system, and they will try to tear it down. There is no rhetoric in what I am saying; it is a simple fact. If it happens, it will mean that our streets would be forever stained with the blood of our best young sons and daughters.

Whenever I speak to student groups, the first question they ask me is "Can't you do something about the war?" The next one usually is "How can you stand to be part of this system?" They mean, "How can you stay in Congress and keep talking about progress, about reconciliation, after all that this society has done to you and your people?" It is the hardest question I could be asked, and the answer is the most important one I can offer. I try to explain to them:

"You can be part of the system without being wedded to it," I say. "You can take part in it without believing that everything it does is right. I don't measure America by its achievement, but by its potential. There are still many things that we haven't tried — that I haven't tried — to change the way our present system operates. I haven't exhausted the opportunities for action in the course I'm pursuing. If I ever do, I cannot at this point imagine what to do next. You want me to talk to you about revolution, but I can't do that. I know what it would bring. My people are twelve percent of the population, at most fifteen percent. I am pragmatic about it: revolution would be suicide."

What is the alternative? What can we offer these beautiful, angry, serious, and committed young people? How are we all to be saved? The alternative, of course, is reform — renewal, revitalization of the institutions of this potentially great nation. This is our only hope. If my story has any importance, apart from its curiosity value — the fascination of being a "first" at anything is a durable one — it is, I hope, that I have persisted in seeking this path toward a better world. My significance, I want to believe, is not that I am the first black woman elected to the U.S. Congress, but that I won public office without selling out to anyone. When I wrote my campaign slogan, "Unbossed and Unbought," it was an expression of what I believe I was and what I want to be — what I want all candidates for public office to be. We need men and women who have far greater abilities and far broader appeal than I will ever have, but who have my kind of independence — who will dare to declare that they are free of the old ways that have led us wrong, and who owe nothing to the traditional concentrations of capital and power that have subverted this nation's ideals.

Such leaders must be found. But they will not be found as much as they will be created, by an electorate that has become ready to demand that it control its own destiny. There must be a new coalition of all Americans — black, white, red, yellow and brown, rich and poor — who are no longer willing to allow their rights as human beings to be infringed upon by anyone else, for any reason. We must join together to insist that this nation deliver on the promise it made, nearly 200 years ago, that every man be allowed to be a man. I feel an incredible urgency that we must do it now. If time has not run out, it is surely ominously short.

921   2876v

B
CHIS   Chisholm, Shirley
HOLM   Unbought and
                    unbossed

DATE			
MAR 2 '99			